The (ex)Crook's Cook Book For Success:

A Prisoner's Guide to Success on the Inside and Out

If you stumble, find the root cause and move on. Don't let yourself get wrapped up in guilt, anger, or frustration, because these emotions will only drag you further down and impede future progress. Learn from your missteps and forgive yourself. Then get your head back in the game and violently execute."
– Brent Gleeson, *Embrace the Suck: The Navy SEAL Way to an Extraordinary Life*

"And once the storm is over, you won't remember how you made it through, how you managed to survive. You won't even be sure, whether the storm is really over. But one thing is certain. When you come out of the storm, you won't be the same person who walked in. That's what this storm's all about."
– Haruki Murakami

"Midway upon the journey of our life I found myself within a forest dark"
– Dante Alghieri, *Dante's Inferno*

"Some beautiful paths can't be discovered without getting lost."
– Erol Ozan

List Of Ingredients

To Jude,

To the last one of the homies that played with oxy's not knowing it was going to rule our foreseeable lives. To the charismatic one, to the one that owns the room. I hope you take the time to heal yourself. To just sit, quiet and let all the thoughts and feelings run out. Silently, calmly working your way through your shit until you're left with the inevitable fact that you're in pain, something's wrong and you need to do something about it. That you can do something about it. It can't keep going on like this, your poor body going through the ringer from all the turbulence in your head. Sit, be quiet with yourself, be still. Work your way through your life, work on understanding your emotions and how you work internally and socially. Do this work with a sober mind and open heart. Forgive yourself for the things you've done and for the things others have done to you. You've not been abandoned, let go of the resentment and realize your drug use and erratic behavior has alienated you, but everyone still cares about and loves you. Please, don't give up on yourself, you can still have an incredible turn-around!

How To Use This Book

The message in this book is simple: heal, plan, and execute. Putting it into practice and changing your life is likely one of the hardest things you'll ever do. It's heavy stuff, and doing the exercises in this book takes time, devotion, and a lot of mental energy. A good way to approach it is to read through it lightly. Take it in on the surface; get an idea of the subjects, what it asks of you, and what it can give you. Then read through it a second time, slowly, taking each section to heart. Pick it back up from time to time to get a refresher.

This book is about you using your time in prison to transform yourself into a better person so you can live a life you'll be proud of. Although this book is based on my experience, it's not about me, it's about you and helping you make your prison experience positive. At times I struggle with taking an authoritative stance on some of subjects because, to be honest, I still struggle with them. This is why I use a lot of excerpts from other authors that I feel are much more knowledgeable and qualified to speak on the concepts this book deals with. I remember during my two-year stint, looking at quotes was one of my favorite things to do, they really resonated, so there is no shortage of quotes in here. I also included definitions to a lot of words because I remember the frustration of not being able to look things up if I didn't know the exact meaning.

When you see the "2¢" symbol, that's me talking about my own experience with the subject. I get a lot of joy and satisfaction from teaching and helping people and that's what this book is about. I hope this book helps you get through and make the most of your time. I hope you use this valuable time to transform yourself and hit the streets a new and improved version. Maybe someday this book can include your success story to help motivate and give hope to others that are going through what you overcame.

A Little About the Author

I grew up middle class in the suburbs —athletic, popular, decent looking, and by all means, I had a lot of things going for me. My dad had a bit of a temper and yelled a lot. My parents fought. There came a day when the fighting was too much, and my parents decided to divorce; I was 15. During the last supper we had as a family, my parents asked my brother and me to choose who got to keep the house and raise us. After that dinner I went to my buddy's house and smoked weed for the first time, I laughed so hard I cried. It was a welcome escape from the shitty feelings of the dinner. I didn't know it at the time, but instead of processing and dealing with the situation and the tough emotions, I was running from them, pretending it hadn't happened. I continued daily marijuana use after that and never really dealt with the painful emotions, not to mention I never chose my mom or dad... Eventually, my dad just moved out after a couple of weeks.

Along with the weed, I started drinking too. In retrospect, whenever I was dealt a tough situation or faced negative emotions, my go-to way to cope with it was to just "get fucked up" and totally avoid it. This pattern continued into my college years. One summer after a difficult breakup, I found myself hanging out with my high school buddies, and they asked me if I wanted to throw in on some Oxys... "Sure," I said. Again, in the midst of a tough situation, I was using chemicals to feel good at a time when I probably should've just felt like shit for a little while. I didn't realize it at this time either, but I was training myself to want to feel good instantly with chemicals while I was going through some shit. I continued to use Oxy daily after that. I held jobs and made my way through college, hiding my addiction for the most part.

Then Purdue stopped making Oxycontin and like countless others I started using heroin. I managed to quit occasionally, but whenever I found myself in a moment of weakness and felt shitty, I just wanted to escape. I'd think, "Just this once." Before I knew it, I was back in the cycle. I was running. I didn't want to face my shit. I lied to my family and friends, told them I'd graduated college (I didn't), and moved out to North Dakota to join the oil boom and make some money. I was able to stay clean for a while, but after burning out from 100-hour work weeks and needing an escape, I got drunk and tried meth. To neutralize the effects of meth and shrink my pupils to a non-suspicious size, I began mixing meth and heroin. It didn't take long for the old "meth-throw" to take effect, and I threw everything away. I couldn't hold jobs anymore and began stealing. I was running faster and harder than I ever had before. In the back of my mind, I knew I was going to end up doing some time, so I stopped giving a fuck. Deep down I think I wanted to get caught. I was running and diving head-first to rock bottom.

Eventually, I fell asleep in a stolen pickup and got welfare called. I woke up to 7-8 police officers ripping me out of the truck. I resisted and fought like hell... I got tazed multiple times, knee strikes were administered. It wasn't the taser or the knee strikes or my face slamming the pavement, it was the pressure one of the officers was putting on the back of my knees that completely subdued me. The pain sent signals to my brain to give up, and I still remember vividly the moment that I screamed out: "OKAY, I'M DONE! GET OFF MY FUCKING KNEE!" (I always enjoyed a good tussle with the boys, and even when outnumbered, I always managed to put up one hell of a fight.) When they picked me up, slammed my bloody face onto the hood of the cruiser, and began reading me my rights, **I'd never taken such a deep sigh of relief in all my life... I knew at that moment that *I was done running.*** I was finally going to take a long, hard, deep look at and into myself and face all the things I'd been running from my whole life. I was gonna do some real time, and that time was going to be spent exorcising my inner demons and confronting my past, confronting my shadow.

What's laid out in this book is the recipe I used to heal and achieve lasting change. The thought exercises and experiments in this book are the same ones I did while doing my two years. I've been out roughly five years now, and I can sum it all up and share with you how I used my time behind bars to change my outlook on life and transform myself into a better person.

I hope you can use this book to make your stay in prison a time of healing and positive transformation, so that when you get out, you're a better version of yourself, a brand-new man, with a definite plan. (Written January, 2023).

A Letter to the Boys

I'd been to jail a few times, just a few weekend stays, then I tried meth. A crime-spree ensued. From a few petty misdemeanors to 13 felonies. A naïve young man raised by a good Christian woman who always said to tell the truth, so I did. "Yep, I did that, did that one too, yep did that." Ratted on myself. Some said it was dumb, and maybe it was, but ya know what? I don't regret it. I didn't have to worry about them bringing on more charges, it felt good to just confess, get a clean slate (in my mind) and move the fuck on. I repented my sins you could say. I could've stayed and fought for a better deal, but I took the first one they threw at me: 10 years, 6 suspended. I heard there was a badass weight room at the minimum-security facility, softball tournaments, handball and all you can eat peanut butter for breakfast, hell fuckin yeah boys, Prisney-land! Nah, I was fuckin terrified, but excited to start the next chapter.

I was in county for six months. Somewhere around the four month mark my thinking wasn't as erratic, I was less stressed, less anxious. I was getting more stable and able to regulate my emotions more and more each day. I was self-healing and for the first time in a really long time I started feeling hopeful about my future. I knew that when it was all over, I was going to have my head on straight and get a second chance at life. Prior to the meth and heroin fueled nose-dive to rock bottom, I always had the delusion that I was in control and was going to stop and get my shit together after that bag. I had the "last bag" in my pocket for 9 years. Quitting, relapsing, running, and wasting my precious time on earth. When I finally had about six months of sobriety under my belt, I woke up to the fact that I was deluded the whole time, I was not in control, the true me- the person I really wanted to be was living in hell...in prison. I was ruled by fear, doubt, insecurity and self-limiting beliefs that I picked up in my childhood. My use of drugs stunted my emotional growth, I was stuck and letting the traumas of my past affect every thought I ever had and every action I ever took.

This book is about finding freedom in prison.

Yes, prison is where I went to become a free man. If you let it, this book can help you find your freedom too. Freedom from living life in a mental prison where the only relief or way to cope is by using drugs or other vices. This might sound corny, but then again, I'm a corny motherfucker! I love you. I don't know you, but I love you, I do. We are brothers in the struggle. I was down and out. I've been where you are; locked up and starting all over in life with a "felon" label. I'm here to tell you: It's possible to turn it all around in there. I know, because I did it. It starts with healing: finding forgiveness and replacing the hate, resentment and negativity in your heart with positivity and love. Then comes the work on re-wiring your brain and neural circuitry to be a positive person that sees and thinks about things differently. Once you see through a new set of eyes, you'll think differently and then you'll act differently, you'll become a whole new person with more possibilities in life. You can dream up a new life and make plans, and because of your freshly healed heart, re-wired brain and new, positive outlook, it'll be possible to execute and achieve. A life you never thought possible, truly is. And there you have it: Heal, Plan, and Execute, as simple as that! It'll only be the second hardest thing you ever do. The hardest of course would be living the rest of your life in that mental prison and squandering this precious life. I hope these words find you at exactly the right place and time and help you make positive and lasting changes.
Love, Swiv

To those doing life who may never see the streets again:

I apologize if a lot of the content of this book is about preparing to re-enter society. I hope you can still find the content useful and helpful and are able to use the framework to create a fuller, more meaningful life no matter where you are.

P.S. To me, the ultimate outcome is MF's getting out and chasing their dreams and then we add their story to the book and this becomes a volume of post-prison success stories.

MINDFULNESS

Mindfulness, mindfulness, mindfulness. You are going to see this word over and over throughout this book, so it's good to start with a clear definition to avoid doubt and confusion later on.

Mindfulness refers to a state of being present and fully engaged in the current moment, without judgment or distraction. Mindfulness is the essential human ability to be fully present, aware of where we are and what we are doing, thinking about, and not overly reactive or overwhelmed by what's going on around us. The goal of mindfulness is to wake up to the inner workings of our mental, emotional, and physical processes. Mindfulness is available to us in every moment, whether through meditation and body scans or mindful moment practices like pausing and breathing.

"Mindfulness isn't difficult, we just need to remember to do it."
-Sharon Salzberg

"Mindfulness does not erase negative memories; it 'transcends' them giving us back our deepest power which resides in our hearts."
- Christopher Dines

"Mindfulness is the aware, balanced acceptance of the present experience. It isn't more complicated than that. It is opening to or receiving the present moment, pleasant or unpleasant, just as it is, without either clinging to it or rejecting it."
- Sylvia Boorstein

"With mindfulness we have the choice of responding with compassion to the pain of craving, anger, fear and confusion. Without mindfulness we are stuck in the reactive pattern and identification that will inevitably create more suffering and confusion."
- Noah Levine

Intro to The Crook's Cook Book

The (ex) Crook's Cook Book for Success is written for inmates by a former inmate. The main objective is to get inmates to use their prison time constructively for healing, self-improvement, self-mastery and creating a plan for their life. The content of the book draws heavily on an overarching theme of self-help books and Stoic philosophy: to turn obstacles, setbacks, and failures into something positive; a learning experience, a blessing in disguise.

"Every adversity, every failure, every heartache carries with it the seed of an equal or greater benefit."
– Napoleon Hill

Adopting a positive mindset can allow you to turn one of the greatest failures (going to prison) into a launchpad for a whole new you. You can turn those lemons into lemonade. You can truly use doing time for what it is intended: to rehabilitate and correct yourself, to re-wire your brain, to break the cycle of destructive tendencies that got you in there in the first place, to master yourself, to alter the path of your life for the better, and to reach your full potential.

The conditions of being locked up: confinement, detachment, solitude, and disconnect are what makes it so hard and painful. But from a positive point of view, these conditions present stillness, quiet, and a unique opportunity to deeply heal your inner wounds and learn to forgive and love yourself. You can daydream with a purpose. You can overhaul yourself and make future plans with a whole new outlook on life. You can re-enter society with a renewed sense of self, execute the goals and plans you made during lockup and live a value-driven life with purpose.

The CCBFS is the book I wish I would have had when I was locked up. It is a seemingly simple message; use your time locked up to heal, improve, make plans, set goals, then when you get out, execute your new goals.

Welcome

So, you fucked around and wound up in jail or prison. No matter the reason, you're there and you can't leave. You can dwell on how bad it sucks and lay around feeling bad for yourself. You can blame it on someone or something else, or on the circumstances. You can glorify the battle stories, network, develop new connections, and plan to be a better criminal. You can tell yourself you're done with all that and lay around watching TV all day, waiting until your release date. The truth is, all those options are a waste of the valuable time you have available to you now that you're locked up. If you can adopt the attitude that maybe you needed a time-out, that maybe you were not on your true path, and that perhaps you need to change your ways, then being locked up presents a unique opportunity for putting in some life-changing work. There *is* a silver lining to being in prison. A lot of good can come from this experience, but it's all in how you see things. Perception is key. This time you're doing can be used to completely transform you into a better version of yourself.

This is the perfect time to adopt a new mindset and develop new thought patterns. This is the time to master yourself and turn your life around.

"Welcome negative experiences, challenge yourself and discipline your mind to be the mentally toughest version of yourself. It will pay off in ways you can't even dream or imagine."
– Andrew Medal

As scary and uncertain as doing time is, it can also be a positive experience. Use it wisely.

All the things that make doing time shitty also make it an ideal environment for putting in work on yourself. You have no responsibilities and there are no outside distractions. You can't leave, and you're forced into solitude, alone with your thoughts. If you know how to courtesy flush, stay out of the day-to-day drama, and respect the boundaries of other inmates, you've got yourself the perfect conditions for resting an exhausted and weary soul. Block out the noise, and prison can give you the stillness and quiet required for introspection, reflection, and deep inner work. Herein lies the unique opportunity that jail, and prison time can offer; **uninterrupted, pure focus on the *self*.**

"It is in this stillness that we can be fully present and finally see truth. It is in this stillness that we can hear the voice inside us."
-Ryan Holiday

Think about it. On the outside, if you take a break from the daily responsibilities of life like paying rent, the bills, going to work, and maintaining relationships with family, friends, and co-workers, everything crumbles. You lose your job, get evicted, and relationships suffer. Daily responsibilities exert constant pressure on you, and as a result, self-care, self-improvement, and mental and emotional health end up at the bottom of your priority list, likely not getting the attention they require. When you're stuck in the vicious cycles of daily life, your job, financial responsibilities, and relationships take precedence over everything else, and your mental and emotional health suffer the consequences. In prison, the absence of life's pressure and responsibilities allows you time to focus all your mental, physical, and spiritual energy on thinking, meditating, healing, improving, and planning out your life.

"A second line of research has shown that economic stress robs us of cognitive bandwidth. Worrying about bills, food, or other problems leaves less capacity to think ahead or to exert self-discipline. So, poverty imposes a mental tax."
– Nicholas Kristof

The fast pace and constant pressure of life imposes a high mental tax, but it is non-existent inside those walls.

Prison can also serve as a great place to re-invent yourself and begin thinking and acting in new ways. You can learn to respect and love yourself, and you can learn to become totally self-reliant. You can practice healthy routines and start using exercise as a healthy foundation to build your new life on. You will probably encounter a lot of tough situations, but ultimately, they will make you mentally tougher, and give you opportunities to build character and strength. You can come out of this situation a better, stronger, wiser, more confident version of yourself.

One of the greatest skills you can have in life is the ability to turn something negative into a positive. Having a positive mental attitude throughout all of this and learning to spin negative shit into a positive is a valuable skill that can benefit you during your stay in prison and for the rest of your life. Try to begin seeing this as an opportunity in disguise. Become mindful of your approach to it, decide to take control of the situation, and turn it into a positive.

So, what kind of person are you going to be in the face of this adversity?

"What matters most is not what these obstacles are but how we see them, how we react to them, and whether we keep our composure."
– Ryan Holiday, *The Obstacle Is the Way: The Timeless Art of Turning Trials into Triumph*

"What matters most is how well you walk through the fire."
– Charles Bukowski

"Opportunity... It often comes in the form of misfortune or temporary defeat."
– Napoleon Hill

"When life gives you lemons, make lemonade."

Prison is the ultimate lemonade factory.

Time to make some fuckin lemonade.

Memento Mori & Your Death

Memento Mori is a Latin saying translated as: "Remember, you must die." The saying is believed to originate from ancient Roman times and fits in with Stoic philosophy.

Memento Mori is the practice of being mindful of your death and remembering that your life will someday come to an end. You are going to die. It's inevitable. The more comfortable you become with this fact, the more fearless you can live your life. Instead of fearing and living in denial about your eventual death, you can use the fact that it's coming as a motivator to live life to the fullest each day, knowing that you're working towards a content and honorable death. Putting some thought towards death can be a healthy exercise and help put things in perspective.

Memento Mori can be very useful to remember in moments of fear and doubt. The trivial fears that can prevent you from taking chances and risks seem insignificant when you compare them to the feelings of having regrets at the time of your death.

This is your death. The first thought experiment is the death exercise. Prison and jail are very helpful in this exercise because when you're locked up, you are sort of dead to the world (it feels like that, anyway). For the purpose of this exercise, pretend that the day you got locked up was your death. Think about what your legacy would've been, what people would say about you, and how you'd be remembered. Picture what your funeral might look like, and think of the emotions of those closest to you after finding out you died.

Write your obituary. Think about what your obituary would say if you died right now. Take it a step further and write your own obituary. Did you do anything meaningful with your life? Will you be remembered as a good person? Did people love you or hate you? Was your life a great success, or a painful tragedy? What were the things that were the most important to you? What did you value and care about most? Did you live a productive and meaningful life? This can be a very powerful exercise. It can bring up some strong and difficult emotions. Don't run from the tough emotions if you experience them. Instead, feel the emotions and the thoughts that accompany them, let them surface. It doesn't feel good, and that's the point. Having negative thoughts and emotions when examining your life means you are not happy with the way you have lived so far. Own that shit and honor it. Let it feel so shitty that you vow to not feel that way again.

What are your regrets? The purpose of this exercise is to point out that although you have probably done many things that you are not proud of, they are usually not high on the list of regrets. Chances are that most of your regrets are the things you *didn't* do. You're now left to wonder: "What if I had done that?", "If only I would've had the courage to do those things", "If only I didn't give in to my fears and doubts." You're left to wonder about the risks you wish you would've taken but didn't out of fear, the way your insecurities and doubtful self-talk steered you away from what you truly wanted to do. This is a powerful concept and should be internalized deeply.

Most regrets come from the things we didn't do, not from the things we did.

Going forward, Memento Mori can be used to remind you that if you continue living your life the way you have been, it's very possible that you'll be left with feelings of regret, wishing you'd done more, risked more, put more on the line, and lived more courageously when you look back on your life.

The good news is that you aren't actually dead and that you can learn from this. Life's ultimate goal is to lie on your deathbed without regrets, feeling proud of a life well lived. Thinking about your death can be a source of motivation when things get tough or when you're facing self-doubt. Whenever you are dealing with negative and self-limiting emotions, remember the regret you felt during these exercises, and use it to fuel your courage going forward. Think of yourself at 90 years old on your deathbed with a sense of accomplishment and contentment, knowing you gave it your all. Use the feeling of regret to reinforce the desire to live a more meaningful life once you're out, so you're not filled with the same regrets when you face your actual death. This is the essence of Memento Mori.

2¢ *This was one of the first mental exercises I did during my time locked up. I was too ashamed and overwhelmed to call anyone on the outside, instead I just pretended I was dead. I sat and slept and let myself feel completely alone and began thinking about my life up to that point. I thought about what a tragedy my life would have been if I really did die. What really hurt was thinking about all the things I didn't do, the wasted opportunities and chances, The feeling of regret was almost unbearable. I internalized that feeling and very early on I started making a deal with myself to not feel this way at the actual end of my life, also realizing making it to old age is not guaranteed and the clock is always ticking. Every day should be spent taking chances, getting outside of the comfort zone and living life to the fullest.*

"Let us prepare our minds as if we'd come to the very end of life. Let us postpone nothing. Let us balance life's books each day...The one who puts the finishing touches on their life each day is never short of time."

– Seneca

"Each time I fail to think about death, I have the impression of cheating, of deceiving someone in me."

– Emil Cioran

"We're all going to die, all of us, what a circus! That alone should make us love each other but it doesn't. We are terrorized and flattened by trivialities, we are eaten up by nothing."

– Charles Bukowski

Healing

Healing: The process of making or becoming sound or healthy again.

The process of returning to ourselves and our natural state of well-being — one where our mind, body, and soul are aligned. Healing is not linear, and it never truly ends. It's an ongoing process. We can encourage our own healing by taking up practices that restore balance to our bodies, minds, and souls.[1]

Healing means facing the most painful emotions and letting yourself feel them. Healing is revisiting the past and replaying the most hurtful memories over and over until you think you have it figured out.[2]

Healing is an active process that requires your presence, participation, and commitment. Healing may require change, growth, and alignment of both your inner and outer worlds, which may require considerable time, dedication, and focus and still does not guarantee any outcome.[3]

Healing takes away the power of pain that makes avoidance seem necessary and allows you to sit with the discomfort. You're able to take accountability. Taking accountability does not mean taking the blame, it means understanding the impact of your own actions on yourself and others.[4]

Healing is at the root of your transformation. Healing is where the journey begins. It all starts way deep within you, at your very core, your innermost self. Fix what is inside you, root out the darkness in your heart, and you will shine on the outside.

To help gain a greater understanding of who you are and how you got that way, the Healing sections are comprised of thought exercises that draw heavily on your past experiences. Although you cannot change what has happened in your past, you can change the way you view, feel and think about it. If you can change your perception, you can change the way you feel and think about things. And if you can change your thoughts and feelings, you can change your actions. Changing your perception is the first step to changing and transforming yourself.

Perceive > Feel > Think > Act

Somewhere along your journey, you were probably hurt, traumatized, stomped on, degraded, humiliated, and beaten or broken down. Chances are, if you didn't deal with and confront these painful events in a healthy manner at the time, they are probably still buried deep within you, and they could still be affecting you to this day. The goal of the Healing section is to address, root out, and deal with this pain so that it no longer negatively affects you.

Emotional pain cannot kill you, but running from it can. Allow. Embrace. Let yourself feel. Let yourself heal."
– Vironika Tugaleva

This is the shitty part. This is the part where you focus your mental energy on your past. Mindfully digging up all the pain and dirt you carry with you and taking a hard look at your inner workings. You will attempt to recall all the bad and traumatic events of your life in order to better understand who you are and why you think the way you do. You'll also root up and discover the presence of any trapped emotions that might be hiding in your heart or subconscious mind and are holding you back from your true potential. By replaying your life as if it were a movie, you can objectively screen yourself and decide what aspects of you need to be accepted, and which negative qualities need to be addressed and changed. You will also learn about the concept of neuroplasticity and how it is at the heart of change. Healing is not easy or fun, but it can be extremely rewarding.

The hardest things are often the most worthwhile.

Think of Andy Dufresne in *Shawshank Redemption*, crawling through the shit pipe, covered in shit, breathing in shit fumes, but alas, he reaches the end, rinses off in the river, and earns his freedom.

You too have to crawl through your own mental shit pipe, as hard and painful as it is, afterwards you're squeaky clean and free from the shit.

Another aspect of the healing section is character-based work which focuses on self-improvement and self-mastery. While critiquing yourself and pointing out all your weaknesses, faults, errors, and other negative aspects, you will also try to find positive replacements to create the best version of yourself. Try to gain a fresh perspective and let the new version of yourself be a positive one. If you can keep your outlook and the way you see things positive, you will begin re-wiring your brain and you'll begin to develop new neural networks that are healthy and sustainable. It's almost like wiping an old hard drive clean and uploading a whole new operating system on a computer.

Healing is crucial. Every human experiences the same range of emotions (except in sociopath situations). Allow yourself this chance to fix the parts of you that are broken. Even if it was childhood, revisit it with all your mental focus and feeling. Give yourself the gift of mending your broken heart and re-wiring bad circuits. If you learn to self-heal with compassion and understanding, you can break your self-destructive tendencies, unleash your true potential, and open yourself up to loving and being loved by others.

"Healing takes courage, and we all have courage, even if we have to dig a little to find it."
– Tori Amos

"To heal is to touch with love that which we previously touched with fear."
– Stephen Levine

<u>The Work</u>

So, what is "the work"? In this context, it refers to healing, self-improvement, and increasing your emotional intelligence. Introspection. Taking a deep dive into yourself and getting in-depth knowledge of your inner workings. Re-visiting your past; all the major events that helped shape who you are today. Examining all the key relationships in your life to get an understanding of how you act in certain situations. Taking an honest and critical look at yourself. Becoming fully aware of your strengths, weaknesses, fears, insecurities, desires, and motivations. Getting intimate with yourself and being 100% real. Taking a good, hard, long look in the mirror and reflecting on yourself and your life. Going completely inward and sitting with yourself to get to know exactly what and who you are. Forgiving yourself for the things you've done to others and yourself. Accepting and loving yourself despite your weaknesses and shortcomings. This is "the work."

"To know thyself is the beginning of wisdom."
– Socrates

"Not until we are lost do we begin to understand ourselves."
– Henry David Thoreau

"If you want to maximize your total potential... you have to know yourself first."
– Mark McGwire

The Ego

The Ego- A concept in psychology that refers to the conscious part of our personality that mediates between our inner impulses and the external world. It is the part of our personality responsible for our sense of self and our ability to adapt to the demands of the world around us.

The ego is also responsible for many of our higher mental functions such as decision-making, reasoning, and problem-solving. It allows us to perceive, remember, and understand the world around us, and to plan and carry out actions to achieve our goals.[5]

Beware the ego!

If we don't allow ourselves the opportunity to heal in a healthy way and correct the narrative/voice in our head, the wounded ego learns to compensate by protecting the painful bits of ourselves in defensive, reactive, and dysfunctional ways. An unhealthy ego is like a shield protecting us from the outside world, but also preventing us from true growth and full potential. The ego can be affected by trauma and shield you from feeling the pain, embarrassment, and hurt you have endured in the past. A wounded ego can do all sorts of tricky things to protect itself. One of its strategies is keeping you in your comfort zone, hindering your progress and growth. The ego is a mixture of both conscious and subconscious forces, and when working on changing your thoughts and behaviors, it is crucial to be aware of the ego's role in your thinking and decision-making.

"Just one thing keeps ego around: comfort. Pursuing great work is often terrifying. Ego soothes that fear, it's a salve to that insecurity, replacing the rational and aware parts of our psyche with bluster and self-absorption. Ego tells us what we want to hear, when we want to hear it.... Only when free of ego and baggage can anyone perform to their utmost."

– Ryan Holiday, *Ego Is The Enemy*

"A bad day for the ego is a good day for the soul."
-Robin Sharma, The 5 AM Club

Sub-Conscious vs. Conscious-Self

The conscious mind is the part of our mind that is actively aware of our experiences and is responsible for our cognitive functions. Consciousness refers to our immediate awareness of our thoughts, emotions, and surroundings. It is the state of being awake and aware of our surroundings and experiences. Our conscious mind is responsible for our logical thinking, decision-making, and problem-solving abilities. We use our conscious mind to actively process information, make choices, and respond to the world around us, while the subconscious mind is a part of our consciousness that operates below the level of our awareness. It includes all mental processes that occur automatically and without our conscious efforts such as instincts, habits, and automatic responses to stimuli.

The subconscious mind is often described as a vast storehouse of information and experiences, including the memories, emotions, beliefs, and desires that influence our thoughts, feelings, and behaviors. It is believed to be responsible for a wide range of mental processes such as creativity, intuition, and problem-solving. It can also influence our physical health and well-being.

Many experts in the field of psychology and neuroscience believe that the subconscious mind plays a significant role in shaping our behavior and experiences, and that by becoming more aware of it, we can gain greater insight into our thoughts, feelings, and actions.

While our conscious mind can only process a limited amount of information at a time, our subconscious mind can process vast amounts of information simultaneously. It can also process information faster than our conscious mind and can perform automatic tasks such as breathing and walking. [6]

Becoming aware of your subconscious mind takes... mindfulness, but once you learn how to do it, it can be a useful skill and tool for learning how to control your thoughts and behaviors. Learning how to access your subconscious plays a huge role in self-mastery.

Trapped Emotions

The emotional "baggage." Shit that happened in your past and that became buried deep inside you because you didn't deal with it at the time. Trapped, hidden away from your conscious self, but still hanging around in the background of the subconscious, tucked away. Festering. A cancerous creature of negative thoughts and feelings. If you're in the light, it hangs in the shadows.

Some of the memories and emotions inside you may be easily made aware of by conscious thought. However, some deeper, trapped memories and the emotions tied to them, may still be lingering in your subconscious. Locked away in the vault. The ego has a way of blocking out painful memories to protect itself, but this can hinder growth and progress. The self-defense mechanisms of the mind that are supposed to protect you can end up becoming a barrier for self-development and personal growth.

Trapped emotions occur when trauma is experienced and not dealt with in a healthy way at the time. Negative emotions may get swept under the rug, denied with substance abuse to cope with or deny these emotions. Chances are you probably have trapped emotional baggage from the trauma you encountered during your upbringing that you didn't process, understand, or heal wholly from at the time. If left undealt with, you will be affected by the trauma, leaving you with a distorted worldview and backwards/destructive ways of thinking. It's very likely that all the traumatic situations from your early life play a role in your negative thinking, destructive behavior, fears, and insecurities you have today.

There are different ways you can rid yourself of this trapped emotional baggage, but since you are locked up without many resources, the most practical way to get rid of this emotional baggage is to just sit, think, and completely work your mind through it. You've got nothing but time and thoughts, so put them both to use.

Replay Your Life

Watch it unfold like a movie. Get to know your story. Get to know yourself.

Think of Scrooge, as he travels through time with the ghost of Christmas past watching the events in his early life that were sad and painful. During this process Scrooge gains a better understanding of how he went from an innocent little kid to a calloused, bitter and heartless person. He watches his life unfold and sees the events that helped shape him.

This exercise provides you with the raw data needed to do "the work." Compared to the environment of someone on the streets, prison provides the ideal environment for doing the work. It requires lots of mental effort and focus, and it can be exhausting and painful. Too painful? No. The notion that some memories are better left covered up and buried away is bullshit. Left undealt with they can cause a lifetime of fucked up thinking that affects your life at every level. Confronting and dealing with shit may be uncomfortable and difficult in the present, but the result is a better life for your future self. If you want to improve the quality of your life, you are going to have to confront your past and rip the band-aid off. If you don't, it will always be there in the shadows, lurking in the background, subconsciously affecting your views, attitudes, thoughts, and actions. Reliving your life up to this point will help you pinpoint the traumatic memories of your past. And once you are fully conscious of your past, you will be able to gain a better understanding of why you are the way you are.

Start as far back as you can possibly remember, and think your way back to your earliest memory. Then the next earliest, and so on. How old are you in this memory? What is happening in it? Can you recall the feelings you had at that moment? Can you remember what you were thinking at this moment? How about the others involved in this memory, can you put yourself into their mind and the way they were thinking in these moments? It's important to remain objective and to keep in mind all the other people involved, including their thoughts, feelings, and actions. Try to remember the way you thought about life and how you viewed the world. Of course, it's fun to think about the cool and funny shit that happened to you as a kid, but for the most part, it's the traumatizing and hurtful situations that have the most impact. So, in order for these exercises to be the most beneficial, it's best to focus on all the key traumatic events that occurred in your childhood and early years. Try to remember all the times you cried as a child, all the times you were hurt and scared. Detail and record the most traumatic and hurtful events in your life. This will probably be a mixture of big events and lots of smaller ones. Make a list of these events. Be aware of the subconscious mind's ability to hide painful things from you. This exercise can be difficult, and painful, but although this stuff happened a long time ago, it could still be affecting you negatively to this day.

-Be "objective."

-See things as they really are, not from a personally biased viewpoint.

-Be neutral, understanding all points of view.

Try to feel your emotions in those moments with all your ability. With the power of hindsight, you can judge the earlier version of yourself and discover when and how you picked up thinking errors (when and where you were when you adopted these patterns). It's not fun to relive awful experiences, but this is an important part of the healing process. The goal is to understand how these events and traumas played a role in shaping your current thinking and behavior. Maybe it wasn't even trauma, but a worldview beset on you by a bad role model. Try to dissect the situations and see how they have impacted you throughout your life, then make a point to use this new insight to help you make positive changes to the way you view yourself and the world in the future.

If you were a drug addict, chances are you weren't the best at processing and dealing with difficult emotions. Addicts use drugs for the dopamine hits, the good feelings getting high produces. When using, the brain doesn't process events and emotions in a healthy way. When something traumatic happens, a healthy non-user is going to experience difficult emotions; they will likely feel sadness and any range of negative emotions until they process it and work it out, eventually beginning to feel better after a while. In the same situation, an addict is going to get high instead of dealing with and processing their emotions, seeking an unnatural source of dopamine to let them feel good when they should normally be feeling bad. This event, whatever it may be, is undealt with and gets buried deep within you. If this keeps occurring, the addict has a lifetime of emotional baggage buried and stacked within them. Not having dealt with the past doesn't mean that it didn't happen, and when the addict runs out of drugs and starts sobering up, all the undealt with events, emotions, and feelings that were denied begin to surface. An overwhelming emotional onslaught occurs.

This exercise can serve to help you re-process and deal with the events that were stacked and buried, and that could be weighing you down, holding you back, and distorting your view of the world and yourself. With a clear mind (hopefully), you can now work through your past traumas and start to understand how you operate mentally and emotionally. Be mindful of how these traumas have caused fears and insecurities in you and how they might affect your perception of the world and the way you think and react in certain situations. Some of these events may have been so painful or have left such an imprint on you that they are at the root of every decision you make. While this might keep you safe and out of that certain situation, it can also be holding you back in a lot of ways and limiting your outcome in life. Becoming aware of when, where, and how you picked up bad thinking habits in the past can help you to change and avoid making these same errors in the future.

Doing all this can bring strong waves of emotions that are sad, depressing, and cringe-worthy. Reliving them may induce anxiety, shame, and negative feelings. It's okay. Honor those shitty feelings and work your way through them. Chances are you've been denying yourself to think about and feel these shitty things for your whole life. And maybe you are even denying them the ability to exit your system. The process sucks. It's putting in the work, and it's work because it's not fun or easy. We put in the work cause through this darkness comes the light. A better version of you is on the other side.

Confront your past to control your future.

Hopefully, with the right attitude and mindset, you can conclude that all the shit in your life is nobody's fault. We're all just fucked up, and there's a long line of fucked up shit happening to everyone. Whoever traumatized you was likely traumatized by someone else, and so on, and so on. We all share the same range of emotions and there are just painful moments in life. However, you do have the choice to heal yourself and make a stand to try and stop the chain of pain.

2¢ For the first few months I spent the majority of my time doing this. Looking back at my life and just dissecting the shit out of it. How did the innocent little kid that I used to be turn into a heroin fiend? Where did I go wrong? What events led to me being stuck in this jail cell? I looked back at my life objectively and realized I was afflicted with a low self-esteem. I had negative self-talk, and I had many negative and erroneous thinking habits. I refused to deal with shit thinking it would just go away ... it never did, it just piled up and continued eating away at me until I was fully consumed by it. First and foremost I had a terrible relationship with my Dad and I was angry at him and resentful of him being so hard on me all the time and always yelling. My first love was hard on me - mentally and emotionally abusive, and that left me traumatized and feeling like I didn't deserve love. Eventually I found a great girl that did love me, but I fucked it up and cheated on her and I absolutely hated myself for that. Of course, there's hundreds, maybe even thousands of other memories I went through, but those were key relationships with lots of painful moments and memories that were worth revisiting and noticing how they still affect me. I was eventually able to work my way through them and be at peace with them, myself, everything and everyone.

"It is not events that disturb people, it is their judgments concerning them."
– Marcus Aurelius

"Reject your sense of injury and the injury itself disappears."
– Marcus Aurelius

"If you are distressed by anything external, the pain is not due to the thing itself, but to your estimate of it; and this you have the power to revoke at any moment."
– Marcus Aurelius

Negative Emotions List

Here's a list of negative emotions with their definitions. As you reflect on yourself, see which of these play a role in your life and think of how and why you commonly feel them. Work on discovering the sources of these emotions.

Abandonment: *Physical abandonment* is being left alone, left behind, or deserted (this is the type of abandonment we most often see in childhood). *Emotional abandonment* is a non-physical feeling of being "left behind" such as feeling given up on, withdrawn from, emotionally deserted, or separated from.

Anger: A strong displeasure and belligerence aroused by a real or supposed wrong; wrath. Anger is often used as a cover-up or form of denial for emotions of hurt or fear.

Anxiety: A generalized feeling of uneasiness and foreboding; a fear of the unknown; fear without a subject (e.g., she feels anxious and fearful all the time for no apparent reason).

Betrayal: *To be betrayed* is to have your trust broken, to be deserted, or hurt by a trusted person. *Betrayal of another* is to be unfaithful in guarding or fulfilling a trust; to be disloyal or violate a confidence, to desert someone who trusts you. *Betrayal of the self* is to break integrity; to act against one's morals, to abuse one's body or soul.

Bitterness: A harsh, disagreeable, or cynical attitude. Being angry or resentful because of hurtful or unfair experiences.

Blaming: *Being Blamed* is to be held responsible, accused, or held guilty for something. *Blaming another* is to hold responsible; accuse; find fault with. Putting responsibility on someone or something else to avoid taking responsibility for oneself. This is a key emotion in creating a victim mentality and can cause a deterioration of personal power. *Blaming the self* is finding fault with oneself, which can lead to feelings of self-abuse, depression, etc.

Conflict: *Internal Conflict* is a mental and emotional struggle within the self, arising from opposing demands or impulses (e.g., he was feeling conflicted about whether or not to take the new job). *External Conflict* is to fight; to disagree or be disagreeable; to struggle or battle against; to antagonize. Prolonged strife or struggle. (E.g., she and her ex-husband experience continual conflict about custody of their children).

Confusion: A disoriented feeling; foggy thinking; chaos; lack of distinctness or clearness; perplexity; bewilderment; a disturbed mental state.

Creative Insecurity: Feeling unsafe or untrusting towards the self concerning the creation or development of something —relationships, family, health, money, career and/or artistic endeavors. A feeling of insecurity that arises and blocks the creative process (e.g., writer's block).

Crying: The (often) involuntary act of expressing a strong emotion; a response to pain or suffering (emotional or physical). A response to or expression of helplessness. A physical sensation felt in the throat, chest, and/or diaphragm. Often becomes trapped when one does not allow oneself to cry (i.e., suppressing this reaction or stuffing it down).

Defensiveness: A state of resisting attack or protecting oneself; being sensitive to the threat of criticism or injury to one's ego; being on guard against real or imagined threats to one's person, physical and/or emotional.

Depression: A state of being sad, gloomy, low in spirits, and dejected. Often a secondary emotion caused by "anger turned inward" at the self, feelings of shame, guilt, etc.

Despair: A complete loss of hope; misery; difficult or unable to be helped or comforted.

Discouragement: Feeling a lack of courage, hope, or confidence; disheartened, dispirited. Losing the nerve to try or attempt something.

Disgust: A feeling of loathing; when good taste or moral sense is offended; a strong aversion (e.g., she felt disgusted when the killer was acquitted).

Dread: Fear of something that is about to happen; apprehension as to something in the future, usually real but sometimes unknown (e.g., he dreaded going to the high school reunion and facing the bullies who had tormented him).

Effort Unreceived: When one's work, achievement, attempts, or endeavors are not accepted or recognized; when one's best effort is not considered good enough; a feeling of being unappreciated. Not feeling approved of or validated.

Failure: When one falls short of success or achievement in something expected, attempted, or desired; (e.g., the failure of a marriage or other relationship, being fired, bankruptcy, performing poorly in athletics, art, academics, etc.).

Fear: A strongly distressing emotion aroused by impending danger, evil, or pain; the threat may be real or imagined.

Forlorn: Miserable; sad and lonely by reason of abandonment, desolation, or emptiness; hopeless; forsaken.

Frustration: Exasperation; being stuck or unable to progress; feeling blocked from causing a change or achieving an objective or goal.

Grief: Intense emotional suffering caused by loss, disaster, misfortune, etc.; an acute sorrow and deep sadness. A universal reaction to bereavement. Also, it can be feeling harassed, vexed, or exasperated (e.g., if someone gives you grief).

Guilt: The feeling of having done wrong or committed an offense. Feeling responsible for the harmful actions of another (e.g., abuse, parents' divorce, death, etc.). Often accompanied by feelings of depression, shame, and self-abuse.

Hatred: To loathe; despise; great dislike or aversion. Often comes as a result of "hurt love." Often hatred is of a situation rather than a person (e.g., hatred of someone else's behavior, unjust circumstances, and so on). Self-hatred creates destructive behaviors and illnesses.

Heartache: Anguish and pain of the heart; distress usually as a result of difficulty or sadness in a relationship. Felt like a crushing or burning physical sensation in the chest.

Helplessness: Being unable to help oneself; being without the aid or protection of another. Having little strength or personal power. A common emotion for those suffering from a "victim mentality." Feeling unable to change one's circumstances or state.

Hopelessness: Devoid of hope; having no expectation of good; having no remedy or cure; no prospect of change or improvement.

Horror: A strong emotion of alarm, disgust, or outrage caused by something frightful or shocking (e.g., an event of extreme violence, cruelty, or macabre).

Humiliation: A painful loss of pride, dignity, or self-respect; to feel mortified; embarrassed.

Indecisiveness: The inability to make a decision; wavering back and forth between one choice or another. Stems from distrust of the self or doubting your ability to make a good decision.

Insecurity: A lack of confidence; self-conscious; shy. Feeling unsafe from danger or ridicule.

Jealousy: Resentful and envious of someone's success, achievements, or advantages. Having suspicious fears; fears of rivalry or unfaithfulness. Results from a fear of not being loved and/or from insecurity.

Lack of Control: Lacking restraint or direction; unable to regulate or command; a feeling that someone or something else determines your course.

Longing: To have a strong desire or craving; a yearning or pining; aching for; to miss some-one or something; to want something you do not have (e.g., she longed for a different life).

Lost: Unable to see the correct or acceptable course; having no direction. Feeling *Physically lost* most often has to do with childhood (e.g., being lost in the woods and unable to find your way home). Feeling *Emotionally lost* refers to a feeling of being unable to see the right decision or direction, being unable to find emotional stability (e.g., he felt lost after his wife died. Or, she hasn't done anything with her life and seems really lost).

Love Unreceived: A feeling that love expressed is or has been rejected. Feeling unwanted, not cared for, not accepted; a lack of love where it is desired.

Low Self-Esteem: A low appraisal of one's own worth or value; feeling and focusing on one's flaws; holding a feeling of disrespect for the self; not confident; lack of self-love.

Lust: Intense sexual desire or appetite; an overwhelming want or craving (e.g., lust for power); passion; to covet.

Nervousness: Unnaturally or acutely uneasy or apprehensive; fearful; timid; to feel jumpy or on edge.

Overjoy: Intense delight or elation which is too overpowering for the body; joy that is a shock to the system.

Overwhelm: To be overpowered in mind or emotion; extreme stress; feeling overpowered with superior force; feeling excessively burdened.

Panic: A sudden, overwhelming fear that produces hysterical behavior, unreasonably fearful thoughts, or physical symptoms such as trembling and hyperventilation; a strong feeling of impending doom.

Peeved: Irritated; annoyed; exasperated; irked; aggravated; ticked off.

Pride: An overly high esteem of oneself for some real or imagined merit or superiority; van-ity (an excessive desire to be noticed, praised, or approved); feeling better than others; haughty; unteachable; has to be right; expects more credit than earned; treats others with disdain or contempt. Having a healthy amount of pride (self-respect or self-esteem) is a good thing, and this type of pride usually doesn't show up as a trapped emotion (although it may show up if one's healthy pride is injured).

Rejection: Feeling denied, refused or rebuffed; discarded as useless or unimportant; cast out; unwanted; forsaken.

Resentment: A feeling of displeasure or indignation at someone or something regarded as the cause of injury or insult; bitter for having been treated unfairly; unwilling to forgive. Often this emotion comes along with animosity (ill will that displays itself in action, strong hostility, or antagonism).

Sadness: Unhappy; sorrowful; mournful; affected by grief.

Self-Abuse: *Abusing the self emotionally* includes negative self-talk (e.g., "I'm such an idiot"), blaming yourself, etc. *Abusing the self physically* includes mistreating the body by use of addictive substances; to not care for the body by lack of sleep, proper diet or nutrition; to work beyond what one can or should endure; to punish or tax oneself excessively. This abuse may help atone for "sins," real or imagined, and is usually driven by anger. Illnesses can be forms of self-abuse (e.g., "I don't deserve to be healed").

Shame: A feeling of being wrong, defective, or disreputable. The painful feeling of having done or experienced something dishonorable, improper, or foolish; disgrace; humiliation; a cause for regret. The lowest vibration of all the emotions. Leads to guilt, depression, and even suicide.

Shock: A sudden or violent disturbance of the emotions or sensibilities; extreme surprise; to feel traumatized or stunned.

Sorrow: A sad regret; distress caused by loss, disappointment, or grief; to feel or express grief, unhappiness, or sadness.

Stubbornness: Being difficult; unbendable; unable or unwilling to forgive; obstinate; headstrong; resistant.

Taken for Granted: Not given thanks for something accomplished, similar to ignored.

Terror: Intense, sharp, overpowering fear; extreme fright; alarm.

Unsupported: A lack of support, help, or encouragement; not provided for by another; not defended when help is needed; feeling the burden is too heavy to bear alone.

Unworthy: Not good enough; beneath the dignity of; not commendable or credible; undeserving; not valuable or suitable; unbecoming.

Vulnerability: Feeling susceptible to harm, either emotional or physical; unsafe; unstable.

Wishy-Washy: Weak, spiritless; undecided; irresolute; without strength of character. To lack conviction; without a backbone.

Worry: Dwelling on difficulty or troubles; unease or anxiety about a situation or a person; extreme concern over potential problems; concern about a loved one in possible distress.

Worthless: Of no importance or value; without excellence of character, quality, or esteem; serving no purpose.[7]

2¢ The following sections consist of the thought processes I took to rid myself of the trapped emotions and old pains that were holding me back and dragging me down. This is the framework I used for letting go of all the emotional baggage I'd been holding onto all my life. I acknowledged all my wrongdoings and accepted that they happened, I got real with myself, no more blinders on, and I saw through what my ego had been hiding from me. I gained a better understanding of myself and how I work. I accepted the harsh reality of the world and this life. It is full of pain and hardship, no matter what you do to avoid it. I remembered the innocent kid I once was and how the pain I endured changed me. I realized that the people who hurt me were hurting too and that they didn't know any better. I came to a place of forgiveness. I forgave those that wronged me, and I forgave myself for all the fucked-up things I'd done and the people I'd hurt. I got rid of the hate and resentment in my heart and I let love in... and it completely changed the way I view the world and myself.

The Art Of Letting Go
Acknowledge, Accept, Understand, Forgive, Love

Truly letting go of all harbored resentments and buried pain and forgiving in your heart is a beautiful feeling. When you let go of all that shit, it creates an opening through which love can enter. (Exercise and journaling can be very helpful for letting go also.)

Acknowledge - To accept or admit the existence or truth of something.

Acknowledge it - Honor it. This is the opposite of denying and burying it. Admit and bring all this old shit up to the surface and confront it with a healthy and balanced mind. It might be uncomfortable at first, but feel the feelings and work through them. Doing this helps to remove the icky negativity from deep within you.

Accept - Believe or come to recognize something as valid or correct.

Accept it – Accept that the things in your past happened and that's just the way it is. At this point it's not good or bad, it just is. There's nothing you can do to change it, but you can change the way you view the circumstances and the effects they've had on you... up to now.

Understand - Perceive the significance, explanation, or cause of something.

Understand it - With a "hindsight is 20/20" mindset, and see the role your past played in shaping you. Use this new understanding of yourself and be compassionate to yourself. Start out fresh now with a greater understanding of how you operate and use this new knowledge to make sure you don't wind up down the same path.

Forgive - Stop feeling angry or resentful towards someone or yourself for an offense, flaw, or mistake.

> *"Forgive them for they know not what they do."*
> **-Jesus (Luke 23:34)**

Forgive- More importantly, forgive yourself. Be kind to yourself, be a friend to yourself, and soften the voice in your head. Forgiveness is the ultimate tool in letting go of all the pain from your past. It is the ultimate act of self-love. Harboring and holding onto negative feelings towards others and yourself keeps the negativity within you. When you're able to fully forgive yourself and others, it releases all the shit you've been willingly or unwillingly holding onto. Figuring out how to truly forgive can lead to an epiphany of the heart. Truly forgiving yourself will lighten your mind, heart, and soul. Forgiveness, in turn, leads to opening the door to let love in.

2¢ During my life replay, I pin-pointed a few key relationships in my life that affected me negatively and one special person that I hurt which also affected me negatively. I had been hanging on to those wounds, hanging on to my self-hatred for causing wounds. I realized though that the people that hurt me didn't do it purposely, and the people I'd hurt wasn't on purpose, we're all just hurting each other and struggling to find our way. I finally understood this and I was able to forgive them, I was able to forgive myself and it was an amazing feeling to let go of all that shit. Forgiveness in particular I think is one of the most powerful things in the world.

> *"The truth is, unless you let go, unless you forgive yourself, unless you forgive the situation, unless you realize that the situation is over, you cannot move forward."*
> **– Steve Maraboli**

Love - An intense feeling of deep affection.

Love - Replace all the negative emotions you've been holding onto with love. Let the love you have for yourself and others overflow.

Here is a section on forgiveness from the book "Trauma: Healing Your Past to Find Freedom Now." Notice how important self-forgiveness is and how different it is from forgiving others.

Trauma - Chapter 10 – Love, Boundaries, and Forgiveness By Pedram Shojai and Nick Polizzi

"True forgiveness is not about the other person or the event, it's about setting ourselves free from the events that happened. Forgiveness is about you, it's self-forgiveness for everything you perceive that you've done wrong because of the trauma, because you have done nothing wrong. You have done the best you could under the circumstances you were given. Forgiveness is about letting go of your self-judgements, self-criticism, and self-hatred. It's time you can release them. The thoughts, feelings and emotions that have ruled your life until this moment are no longer important. What matters is your capacity to forgive yourself so that you can love yourself... as we work toward compassion and forgiveness for ourselves, it opens the door to forgive our perpetrators, not for what they did, but for their own imperfections, struggles and pain. As your self-forgiveness grows you see that the person who abused you was coming from their own deep level of trauma and woundedness. Dr. Paul explained it like this: people who abuse; they don't know what love is, they don't know what compassion is, they're deeply abandoning themselves, they're projecting all their self-loathing onto their child or others. Eventually we get to understand that and to see that they were just coming from their own deep woundedness and we can forgive, we don't forget, we don't condone but it does mean that we're no longer blaming, we're no longer feeling like victims of whatever happened to us and as we reached this place, we began to soften towards others and their experiences of being human and that includes some of the people we have blamed for hurting us or who were responsible for the experience we endured. To resolve the trauma her patients had to have a willingness to self-confront, they had to be willing to look at whatever trauma happened in their lives and ask themselves: where can I take responsibility for this or in my life? Can I see that I'm attracting similar kinds of people or experiences and why could that be? What is it that I need to adjust from there? It can take going through a trauma release therapy such as EMDR, cognitive behavioral therapy or somatic, experiencing whatever treatment is right for them and then eventually getting to forgiveness. I know people aren't going to want to hear about forgiveness, but it is not lip service doctors told us, it's not "oh, I forgive them", there's actually a process I take people through that changes the brain hormones at the way the genetics are expressed. It's hard work and you don't go from A-Z, you have to digest your feelings and experiences the same way you digest your food."[8]

2¢ Hopefully, if you're like me, after reliving your life and reviewing your traumas, you can come to the realization that the people who wronged and abused you were, after all, were only human and dealing with their own shit. Once you realize that everyone's fucked up, it's easier to not take things personally, and it's easier to purge the hate, anger, resentment, and all the other nasty feelings that you may have concerning others and past situations.

"The weak can never forgive. Forgiveness is the attribute of the strong."
– Mahatma Gandhi

"Resentment is like drinking poison and then hoping it will kill your enemies."
– Nelson Mandela

"To be wronged is nothing, unless you continue to remember it."
– Confucius

"Forgiveness has nothing to do with absolving a criminal of his crime. It has everything to do with relieving oneself of the burden of being a victim —letting go of the pain and transforming oneself from victim to survivor."
– C.R. Strahan

"Grudges are for those who insist that they are owed something; forgiveness, however, is for those who are substantial enough to move on."
– Criss Jami, *Salomé: In Every Inch in Every Mile*

Taking an Inventory of the Self

If you're familiar with AA/NA, this is Step #4:

"The purpose of Step 4: making a searching and fearless moral inventory of yourself, is to begin to determine the root cause of one's addiction, identify any weaknesses that may have contributed to addiction, and understand personal strengths that can help support the person with their self-discovery and recovery in the program. Through this moral inventory, the individual will uncover negative thoughts, emotions, and actions that have contributed to the spiraling of their addiction. They will also direct their attention from blaming others to seeing their part in problems created. This step requires humility and rigorous honesty, as being truthful with oneself will be the blueprint for success with sobriety."

"Recognizing the dark side of yourself makes you a more complete individual. It's a profoundly transformative experience."
– Robert Greene

"There will be times in your life when things simply have to be replaced because they are tired, broken, worn out, harmful, outdated, or irrelevant. Take an inventory of the things that no longer serve your best and highest good so you can replace them with things which do."
-Susan C. Young

"In a sense we re-write our past. We change our narrative. We reprogram ourselves. There is no objective history, this we know, only stories. Our character is the result of this story we tell ourselves about ourselves, and the process of inventorying breaks down the hidden and destructive personal grammar that we have unwittingly allowed to govern our behavior"

-Russell Brand

Character Flaws

Character flaw: A negative quality in a character that affects them or others in a detrimental way.

Taking an objective look at yourself is not fun, easy, or comfortable. It takes a level of brutal honesty with yourself to examine your flaws and defects. If in the last exercise, you used the raw data from reliving your life to root out how traumas affect you on an emotional level, now you're taking a look at certain characteristics you've picked up along the way.

"Confront the dark parts of yourself, and work to banish them with illumination and forgiveness. Your willingness to wrestle with your demons will cause your angels to sing."

– August Wilson

You want to be very critical of yourself here, taking an inventory of any weaknesses in your character. Brutal honesty is necessary here. You want to identify the character defects, deepest fears, and insecurities that are limiting you and holding you back. Seek out painful inner truths and deal with them objectively. Some of the traumas from the last exercise may be tangled and intertwined with this part. It's good to have some awareness of the connections between traumas and how they affected your self-esteem and perhaps played a role in creating some of the unwanted qualities you're aiming to change. Replay and remember all the significant personal and professional relationships you've had in your life. Focus on the ones that ended abruptly or badly, and focus on all the memorable fights you've had in your life.

Take a good hard look at yourself and decide what must be changed. This calls for some self-psychoanalysis. You should already be somewhat aware of your shortcomings. But again, the ego can hide these from you, so it's important to be very mindful and thorough.

Again, this is not easy to do, but focus on all your flaws and negative qualities. Be completely, brutally, and totally honest with yourself. If you want to build the best version of yourself, you must first tear down the current one. Facing the hard truths about yourself is the first step to creating a better version of yourself. Try to remain compassionate towards yourself while doing this. It's a delicate balance between being hard on yourself and being understanding and kind to yourself.

"Much as we must keep returning to the gym and pushing weight against resistance in order to sustain or increase our physical strength so we must persistently shed light on those aspects of ourselves that we prefer not to see in order to build our mental emotional and spiritual capacity."

– Jim Moore

Following is a list of some negative character traits. Check these out, be real with yourself, and identify any that you might possess. Think about the "replaying your life" exercise and try to figure out why you have some of these traits. These traits are often ways in which the ego defends itself, deeply rooted in some fear or insecurity. Having become hard-wired habits that are so ingrained in you, you may not even be aware of them. Compassionately criticize your personality and behaviors, and think of the joy that could come to your life if you were able to successfully replace your negative qualities with positive ones. This kind of change is extremely difficult, but with focused attention and mindfulness, it *is* possible to overcome, and you can begin on a new path filled with positivity and love.

Review the list and determine which of these you might possess. (Some of the list overlaps with the list of negative emotions.)

Negative Character Traits

Abusive: Engaging in or characterized by habitual violence and cruelty.

Aloof: Conspicuously uninvolved and uninterested, typically through distaste.

Anger: A strong feeling of annoyance, displeasure, or hostility.

Antagonistic: Showing or feeling active opposition or hostility toward someone or something.

Anxious: Characterized by extreme uneasiness or brooding fear about something yet to happen.

Apathetic: Showing or feeling no interest, enthusiasm, or concern.

Argumentative: Given to expressing divergent or opposite views.

Arrogant: Having or revealing an exaggerated sense of one's own importance or abilities.

Beat yourself up: Overly critical of one's own behavior or actions.

Bigotry: Unreasonable attachment to a belief, opinion, or faction. Particularly prejudice against a person or people.

Blaming: Assigning responsibility for a fault or wrong. Not taking responsibility.

Boastful: Showing excessive pride and self-satisfaction in one's achievements, possessions, or abilities.

Cheating: Acting dishonestly or unfairly in order to gain an advantage.

Closed-minded: Having or showing rigid opinions or a narrow outlook.

Codependent: Excessive emotional or psychological reliance on a partner.

Complaining: A person who expresses dissatisfaction or annoyance about something.

Conceited: Excessively proud of oneself; vain.

Controlling: Maintain influence and authority over.

Cowardice: Lacking the courage to do or endure dangerous or unpleasant things.

Critical: Expressing adverse or disapproving comments or judgments.

Deceptive: Giving an appearance or impression different from the true one; misleading.

Destructive: Causing great and irreparable harm or damage.

Devious: Showing a skillful use of underhanded tactics to achieve goals.

Dishonesty: Behaving or prone to behave in an untrustworthy or fraudulent way.

Egotistical: Excessively conceited or absorbed in oneself; self-centered.

Envious: Feeling discontented or resentful longing aroused by someone else's possessions or qualities.

Excess: An amount of something that is more than necessary, permitted, or desirable.

Fanatical: Obsessively concerned with something.

Favoritism: The practice of giving unfair preferential treatment to one person or group at the expense of another.

Fearful: Feeling afraid; showing fear or anxiety.

Frustration: Feeling of being upset or annoyed, especially because of the inability to change or achieve something.

Gluttony: Habitual greed or excess in eating.

Gossiping: Casual or unconstrained conversation or reports about other people, typically involving details that are not confirmed to be true.

Greed: Intense and selfish desire for something, especially wealth, power, or food.

Harsh: Unpleasantly rough or jarring to the senses.

Hopelessness: A feeling or state of despair; lack of hope.

Ignorance: Lack of knowledge or information.

Impatience: The tendency to be impatient; irritability or restlessness.

Impulsive: Acting without forethought.

Inconsiderate: Thoughtlessly causing hurt or inconvenience to others.

Indecisive: Not having or showing the ability to make decisions quickly and effectively.

Injustice: Lack of fairness or justice.

Insecure: Not confident or assured; uncertain and anxious, not firmly fixed; liable to give way or break.

Insincere: Not expressing genuine feelings.

Intolerance: Not tolerant of views, beliefs, or behavior that differ from one's own.

Irresponsibility: (of a person, attitude, or action) Not showing a proper sense of responsibility.

Isolating: Having the effect of making a person feel or be alone or apart from others.

Jealousy: Feeling or showing envy of someone or their achievements and advantages, suspicion of someone's unfaithfulness in a relationship.

Judgmental: Having or displaying an excessively critical point of view.

Laziness: The quality of being unwilling to work or use energy; idleness.

Liar: A person who tells lies.

Manipulative: Characterized by unscrupulous control of a situation or person.

Meddling: Intrusive or unwarranted interference.

Negative body image: Feeling shame, anxiety, or self-consciousness about one's shape as well as a distorted perception of physical appearance.

Neglectful: Not giving proper care or attention to someone or something.

Opinionated: Conceitedly assertive and dogmatic in one's opinions.

Overcompensating: The taking of excessive measures in attempting to correct or make amends for an error, weakness, or problem.

Perfectionism: Refusal to accept any standard short of perfection.

Pessimism: A tendency to see the worst aspect of things or believe that the worst will happen; a lack of hope or confidence in the future.

Possessive: Demanding someone's total attention and love.

Prejudice: Preconceived opinion that is not based on reason or actual experience.

Procrastination: Delay or postpone action; put off doing something.

Reckless: Without thinking or caring about the consequences of an action.

Remorseful: Filled with remorse; sorry.

Resentment: Bitter indignation at having been treated unfairly.

Rude: Offensively impolite or ill-mannered.

Sarcastic: Marked by or given to using irony in order to mock or convey contempt.

Skeptical: Not easily convinced; having doubts or reservations.

Undisciplined: Lacking in discipline; uncontrolled in behavior or manner.

Unreliable: Not able to be relied on.

Untrustworthy: Not able to be relied on as honest or truthful.

Vengeful: Seeking to harm someone in return for a perceived injury.

Wasteful: (of a person, action, or process) Using or expending something of value carelessly, extravagantly, or to no purpose.

Worry: To give way to anxiety or unease; to allow one's mind to dwell on difficulty or troubles. [10]

"The function of education is to teach one to think intensively and to think critically. Intelligence plus character, that is the goal of true education."
– Martin Luther King, Jr.

"Character cannot be developed in ease and quiet. Only through experience of trial and suffering can the soul be strengthened, ambition inspired, and success achieved."
– Helen Keller

"People grow through experience if they meet life honestly and courageously. This is how character is built."
– Eleanor Roosevelt

"Our character is what we do when we think no one is looking."
– H. Jackson Brown, Jr.

"Such as are your habitual thoughts, such also will be the character of your mind; for the soul is dyed by the thoughts."
– Marcus Aurelius

"The foundation stones for a balanced success are honesty, character, integrity, faith, love, and loyalty."
– Zig Ziglar

Neuroplasticity, Motivation, The Serenity Prayer, and Change

Neuroplasticity - the brain's powerful ability to change itself and adapt.

"Brain plasticity, also known as neuroplasticity, is the brain's ability to change in response to our experiences, at any age. This remarkable ability of the brain is at the heart of learning, moving, thinking, performing, and the quality of our lives."

-Dr. Michael Merzenich

When you learn something new or change a pattern or habit, that's neuro-plasticity at work. Changing habits like quitting smoking, abusing drugs, learning to play an instrument, learning a new language, controlling anger or anxiety, losing weight/exercising, or thinking differently altogether are all examples of neuroplasticity at work. But neuroplasticity is a double-edged sword. As much as it allows us to change and take on new and healthy habits, it also allows us to change in a negative direction. Think of taking that first hit of a drug, becoming addicted, and the downward spiral that ensues. It goes both ways. Neuroplasticity allows us to change, but in what direction we choose to change, this is up to us.

Neuroplasticity is the brain's ability to make new neural pathways. When you try to learn something new or change, you're attempting to create a new neural pathway. Your brain isn't used to it and the new neural net-works have not yet been strengthened enough to be comfortable or be-come your modus operandi. You must continue to repeat the new behavior to create a sufficiently strong neural pathway. Only then can the new be-havior be hardwired in your brain. "If it fires together, it wires together" is a commonly quoted phrase when talking about neuroplasticity. At the be-ginning of learning or changing something it is uncomfortable, and depend-ing on what you're doing, it can be uncomfortable for quite a while. There's a learning curve to everything, and changing habits is no exception. Until those neural pathways are second nature, you must focus, concentrate, and use a lot of mental energy to achieve the new way. And even after, you must remain vigilant to not be tricked into hopping back onto the old neural path, a good example of that is relapsing.

Merzenich found that there are a few things required to create new neural pathways, or in other words, to make changes. In order to fully embrace neuroplasticity, you must:

1) **Be aware of what you want to change or learn.**
2) **Be persistent and remain focused and attentive to what it is you want to change or learn.**
3) **Be properly motivated in order to push through the difficulty and uncomfortable nature of change and learning.**

These elements make up the basic formula for change: being aware of what you want to change, being properly motivated to make that change, and constant focus and repetition of the desired behavior. Having the courage to make that change is a prerequisite. Following through reinforces these pathways to create a lasting new neural pathway, effectively changing your habits.

Trying to learn something new can be very difficult, painful, and frustrating. In that moment when you become so frustrated that you just want to quit; breathe, reset your mind, and make a conscious decision to keep trying and never give up. This is how new neural pathways are built... persistence and patience are key.

"People who get really good at anything just keep reproducing the experience over and over again consciously. They do it so many times that it becomes subconscious. The repetition of any action will neurochemically condition your mind and body to begin to work as one. When you've done something so many times that your body now knows how to do it better than your conscious mind, you've mastered that knowledge. It's a state of being. You know how you do it, but you don't know how you know how any longer, it's automatic. It's natural. It's easy. It's innate in you, you've become it."

– Dr. Greg Reid

"It only takes a moment to make the wrong choice and jeopardize your future. What feels like an insignificant decision today can have a great lasting impact on your

future. Each choice sets a precedent and when you make the same wrong choice several times in a row it becomes your standard modus operandi."
– Martin Meadows

"If you make disciplined, caring choices, you are slowly engraving certain tendencies into your mind. You are making it more likely that you will desire the right things and execute the right actions. If you make selfish, cruel, or disorganized choices, then you are slowly turning this core thing inside yourself into something that is degraded, inconstant, or fragmented."
– David Brooks

Motivation

Motivation - the process that initiates, guides, and maintains goal-oriented behaviors.

To stay focused and strong-willed in tough times, it's essential to be adequately motivated. So, what's your motivation? What do you want most out of life? It's important to know this. Make a clear declaration to yourself that this is what you want to achieve most in life, and that this is what you will spend all your energy and effort on. It must be deeply tied to your core and be a deep, burning desire. This will give you the willpower to blast through walls and obstacles that might otherwise make you quit and prevent you from achieving your goals. Your motivation must be clearly defined to sustain high levels of discipline and keep you motivated while going through difficult and challenging times.

Some Common Motivating Factors Include:

- Money and rewards — most people think that what they want in life is money and the next shiny object, but they don't realize that the material things they want are just a means to an end. Either way, money can be a great motivator, but be aware of the emptiness chasing only money can bring.

- Desire to be the best — some people cannot accept being number two. They fight hard and they work hard because they hate to lose.
- Helping others — some people are motivated by helping others. They want to see changes in peoples' lives and they want to fight for a better future for the world.
- Power and fame — these are the people who are inspired to become leaders and they are driven to achieve great power and fame in life.
- Recognition — this is another factor that motivates certain people. They want to prove that either they are right or someone else is wrong.
- Passion — why do you think most successful people are successful? Why do you think they are willing to wake up early and work harder than ordinary people? The answer is that they are passionate about what they do.
- Love and belonging — these social needs prevent you from feeling isolated or depressed.
- Sex — the term *libido* was coined by Sigmund Freud and used by him to encompass the seeking of pleasure in general, one of the major motivating forces for human activity.

"Desire is the starting point of all achievement."
– Napoleon Hill

So. What do you desire most? Use that to motivate you.

2¢ I use this trick all the time, almost every day. I think about what it is that I want most. Financial freedom, time freedom, a good woman, a family, to help people, self-expression, good health, to build my own home, fast foreign cars, all the things. Those are my desires and I tell myself I will only get those things if I keep my head down and keep grinding on my goals. I delay my gratification and the attainment of these things and keep on grinding and grinding and grinding. I know if I keep this up, eventually I will have an abundance.

The Serenity Prayer

Written in 1932 by Reinhold Niebuhr, the Serenity Prayer embodies Stoic philosophy and highlights the elements needed to change your ways.

Serenity Prayer - "God, grant me the serenity to accept the things I cannot change, courage to change the things I can, and the wisdom to know the difference."

The original version reads, "Father, give us courage to change what must be altered, serenity to accept what cannot be helped, and the insight to know the one from the other."

After all the self-examination that's been done, you should have a good idea of what you need to work on changing, no matter how entrenched it is, and what you must accept, no matter how painful or difficult it is. Hopefully, you've acquired some wisdom and can differentiate between these two groups. Utilize the stillness and alone time to get real with yourself.

Serenity - the state of being calm, peaceful, and untroubled. The prayer asks for you to accept the things you cannot change with a peaceful and calm mind and heart. Be at peace with your shortcomings and learn to love yourself despite them; you are beautiful and worthy of love.

Wisdom - the quality of having experience, knowledge, and good judgment; the soundness of an action or decision with regard to the application of experience, knowledge, and good judgment. This applies to being real with yourself and using sound, honest judgment when deciding what you can change about yourself, and what you must accept.

Courage - the ability to do something that frightens you; strength in the face of pain or grief; the quality of mind or spirit that enables a person to face difficulty, danger, pain, etc., without fear; bravery.

Finally, the serenity prayer calls for courage. The ability to get up and do what you know you must do to change your ways and begin living your life, even if it's hard or scary. Courage is one of the cardinal virtues in Stoicism. Without it, the other virtues crumble. Courage is what you have when your

desire to achieve said change is greater than the fear keeping you from doing it. Courage can be defined as the opposite of fear. There are many types
of courage. Physical courage is like a fireman running into a burning house
to save a victim. Moral courage is sticking up for what is right while no one
else does, risking ridicule and humiliation. Courage is the driving force behind changing your ways. When you rid yourself of fear, insecurity, and
doubt, you'll be left with the courage to begin acting in accordance with
your true potential.

Change

Change- To make someone or something different, alter, or modify.

When you combine proper motivation, the courage to act, and focused attention... you harness your neuroplasticity, and the result is change.

Creating lasting change takes full-on conscious effort, focus, and mindfulness as your new neural pathways are weak and encounter resistance. If
not persistent and on it 24/7, it's still possible to jump back on the old neural pathways and relapse back to your old ways.

It takes a lot of focus at the beginning. It may require meditation and be
your only focus for the entire day, for days on end. However, as these new
neural pathways become stronger, the new method of thinking or acting
becomes more automatic and can almost be done subconsciously or without effort. Think of your brain as a computer to which you're uploading an
entirely new software program. Once it becomes comfortable and second
nature, you can lower the amount of mental energy you once had to put
into learning this new way, and you can change the object of your focus
and concentration to the next pressing objective. Once it becomes hard-
wired and your confidence grows, you can also develop your own unique
style and even become a master in this area.

"The secret to success is to keep pushing and stay focused."
– Bobby Boland

"You have to decide what your highest priorities are and have the courage — pleasantly, smilingly, non-apologetically — to say "no" to other things. And the way to do that is by having a bigger "yes" burning inside."
– Stephen Covey

"Progress is impossible without change; and those who cannot change their minds cannot change anything."
– George Bernard Shaw

Build Your New Self

It is now time to focus on the positive. This is all about replacing negative emotions and traits with positive ones. This will allow you to reinvent yourself. Of course, this type of change is not easy, but if you continue to work on it constantly, you can successfully reinvent yourself.

Ask yourself:

- What kind of person do I want to be?
- What kind of qualities do I respect in other people?
- What kind of person do I want to be remembered as?
- What is the ideal version of myself?

Your answers will help determine who you want your future self to be. Remember, for lasting change to occur, you need to identify exactly what it is you want to change about yourself and then put focus and effort into implementing that change. This type of change does not come quickly or easily, it takes constant work and focus, and you will likely fail many times before real change occurs.

If you've always had a quick temper, for example, it is going to take a long time to learn how to breathe, think clearly, and stay cool in the moment. Learning how to do that is probably going to be the result of many awful feelings that come right after you lose your temper, or in other words; right after a failed attempt at controlling it. Use the frustration to motivate you. Keep at it, don't give up, it is possible to change your behavior. If you stick with it, each time you try and fail you will learn a tiny bit more about your thought processes in the moment, the warning signs, and then one time you might catch it right before it happens by taking a deep breath, or finding some method that allows you to control it. After that breakthrough moment occurs (and it will if you keep trying), you can rejoice in the fact that you successfully controlled your temper. The next time you might even be able to control it again. If you remain mindful, focused, and motivated to control your thoughts and reactions, you will eventually create a new and lasting habit of controlling yourself in situations where the previous version of yourself always lost control. You will become a better version of yourself, and it will be glorious. Stay positive, learn from the failed attempts, and never give up.

2¢ I had a problem with my temper and found a trick that helped. Right before I lose my shit, I say to myself, "I am mad." Somehow, saying it and hearing it out loud snaps me out of seeing red. It's a simple process that has helped me change my behavior. It took many failed attempts before I learned how to use this trick, but I kept trying.

It's important to be mindful of which emotions you decide to feel in certain situations. Perhaps in the past when you got hit with a difficult situation or encountered some type of setback you got angry, felt hopeless, and your first instinct was to get high. Instead of feeling negative when you face a difficult, unforeseen, or painful experience, choose to look for the possible benefit of the situation. Don't run from it, and don't deny it. Keep a positive attitude towards the situation knowing that, although challenging, it can lead to growth and new opportunities. When you adopt a positive mindset like this, you can choose to feel positive emotions rather than negative ones, and it can put you on a path of success rather than self-destruction.

Here is a list of positive emotions you can work on feeling instead of the negative ones your old self may be used to feeling.

Positive Emotions

Admiration: Approval with a dash of awe, often with respect to a person you look up to.

Abundance: This emotion is how it feels when you have everything you need and then some, so much that there's no need to worry you'll run out.

Affection: A warm feeling directed at someone whose company you enjoy; this can be a person or a pet.

Attraction: A strong inner pull toward another person.

Altruism: When you do something good for someone else. It can also be an overwhelming desire to show generosity to others without expecting something in return.

Amusement: Something takes you by surprise and makes you laugh, or when you find yourself pleasantly distracted by something.

Awe: Admiration or gratitude with a touch of reverence.

Bold and Daring: A fearless or fear-defying readiness to step out beyond your comfort zone.

Blissful: A state of intense or increased satisfaction or contentment.

Cheerfulness: Noticeably happy and upbeat, "being in a good mood."

Compassion: A strong sympathy and concern for the sufferings of others.

Confidence: A feeling of calm trust in your abilities or qualities; a certainty that something is true.

Connectedness: You feel consciously linked to all humanity or all living things, so much so that you can't stomach the thought of harming anyone or ignoring their suffering.

Contentment: Genuinely happy and satisfied with your current state of reality.

Curiosity: Compelled to know more about something that has captured your interest.

Dynamism: Feeling you have when you overcome something that once daunted you. Something in you has shifted, and you feel ready for the next challenge.

Eagerness: Passionate readiness to do or experience something.

Elevation: Going above and beyond the normal level of kindness, generosity, and compassion.

Empowerment: Feeling endowed with the power to do something (or anything).

Enjoyment and Delight: Taking pleasure in something or finding joy in it.

Enthusiasm: Energetic and optimistic interest in something.

Euphoria: Intense, giddy happiness or elation.

Excitement: State of agitated or optimistic anticipation, often in regard to something that's about to happen or something you want to do.

Fascination: Intense interest in something that eclipses all else, you ache to know more about it.

Freedom: Feeling of self-determination or of having just been liberated from a type of slavery.

Friendship: Bound to someone by fellowship or mutual understanding.; you like each other well enough to spend time together, and you like the way you feel when you do.

Forgiveness: Letting go of any ill will toward someone who has hurt you and wanting only good for them instead.

Generosity: Giving your resources or yourself to others to help them or show them your love and support.

Gratitude: Showing thankfulness.

Goodwill: Wanting only good things for someone, regardless of whether the feeling is mutual.

Harmony: Feeling at peace with those around you, your mutual respect and love eclipse any differences.

Hopefulness: Hope is more often associated with faith or trust than with arbitrarily choosing to expect everything to turn out well. It goes beyond mere optimism to embrace and hold onto a promise of ultimate happiness.

Happiness: Genuine happiness is a feeling of intense and unshakable well-being regarding your current state of reality.

Importance: You feel a sense of importance when someone acknowledges your value and how critical you are to their success or happiness.

Inspiration: Feeling mentally stimulated to do or to create something.

Interest: Wanting to know more about something or someone that has caught your attention.

Joyfulness: Intense delight or happiness, often because of something that has happened or because of something someone did.

Love: A feeling of profound affection for someone; an intense desire to serve that person's best interest; a desire for a closer relationship.

Momentum: You've got the ball rolling; you're accomplishing things; you feel unstoppable.

Optimism: Confidence that things will work out to your advantage and/or to someone else's.

Passion: You love what you're doing so much that it compels you to continue doing it; there's a fire inside you to continue with your pursuit.

Pride: A deep satisfaction in the accomplishment of something; a strong appreciation for your own worth or dignity.

Relief: The feeling that washes over you when something turns out better than expected.

Revelation: Realizing a profound and life-changing truth (an epiphany).

Romance: Romance happens when you're in love with someone, or when your partner does something romantic for you.

Satisfaction: Gratification and approval with regard to an experience or an occurrence.

Serenity: An unshakable calm or tranquility irrespective of your circumstances.

Spontaneity: Doing something unexpected and spur-of-the-moment.

Surprise (the good kind): A feeling of pleasant astonishment or stunned satisfaction over a sudden or unexpected experience or occurrence.

Triumph: Having achieved a great victory or having prevailed over a challenge.

Unity: Feeling united with someone or with a group of like-minded people; standing as one.

Wholeness: Feeling integrated as if something you lost has returned, or something you were always missing is now part of you.

Worthiness: To feel good enough and deserving of something good. [11]

"You'll reach a new level of freedom when you take control of your emotions."
– Clyde Lee Dennis

"In the world of money and investing, you must learn to control your emotions."
– Robert Kiyosaki

"Any person capable of angering you becomes your master."
– Epictetus

"If you cannot control your emotions, you cannot control your money."
– Warren Buffett

Character Strengths

Try to envision the best version of yourself. What kind of qualities do you want to possess? What kind of qualities do your favorite people have? What kind of person do you want to be remembered as?

What follows is a list of character strengths. Take a look and decide which of these you might already possess and can build on, and which ones you don't have but would like to adopt. If there is a quality that you lack, but in your heart want to possess, think about what it'll take to start displaying that trait. Start experimenting with and practicing being a new person in there... You likely won't see any of these people again so who cares if it's a little unnatural at first? Remember, in order to be that person, you must think like that person, so start at the thought level and you'll begin acting accordingly.

2¢ I began working on being a comedic relief and laughing at myself instead of taking jokes personally in there (There's certainly no shortage of jokesters in prison). It took some time to learn the right moment to jump into a group conversation with something funny, but I started doing it and eventually, it became part of my personality. It was also a difficult adjustment, learning to laugh at myself, but I had a cellmate that was so funny and good at this and I took mental notes and started bypassing the anger route and learned how to lighten up and laugh when I was the butt of a joke.

Character Strength List

Wisdom: The quality of having experience, knowledge, and good judgment; the quality of being wise. The soundness of an action or decision with regard to the application of experience, knowledge, and good judgment.

Creativity: The tendency to generate or recognize ideas, alternatives, or possibilities that may be useful in solving problems, communicating with others, and entertaining ourselves and others. A creative person is clever, original, adaptive, and a good problem solver.

Curiosity: A desire to know; interest leading to inquiry. A curious person is interested in exploring new things, thoughts, or ideas and is open to new ideas or ways of thinking.

Judgment: The ability to reach a decision or opinion after careful thought and consideration. A person with judgment is a critical thinker that thinks things through thoroughly and open-mindedly.

Love of Learning: An intense feeling of deep affection for the acquisition of knowledge or skills through experience, study, or by being taught. A person with a love for learning masters new skills and topics and systematically adds to their knowledge base. A deep passion for learning for learning's sake.

Perspective: The angle or direction from which a person looks at something; point of view; a particular attitude toward or way of regarding something. A person with good perspective is wise, provides wise counsel, and takes the big picture view.

Courage: The ability to do something that frightens you; strength in the face of pain or grief. Comes from the Latin word "cor," meaning "heart."

Bravery: Courageous behavior or character; a person with bravery shows valor, doesn't shrink from fear, and speaks up for what's right; digs deep to find the strength to push through and overcome what might seem impossible.

Perseverance: Persistence in doing something despite difficulty or delay in achieving success. A person with perseverance is persistent, industrious, committed, and finishes what they start.

Honesty: A refusal to lie, steal, or deceive in any way. A person with honesty is authentic, trustworthy, and sincere.

Zest: Great enthusiasm and energy. A person with zest doesn't do things half-heartedly and is full of vibrant energy and enthusiasm.

Humanity: A virtue linked with basic ethics of altruism (the belief in or practice of disinterested and selfless concern for the wellbeing of others). It also symbolizes human love and compassion toward each other. (Wikipedia).

Love: An intense feeling of deep affection. The emotion felt and actions performed by someone concerned for the well-being of another person. A person with love is warm, genuine, and values close relationships.

Kindness: The quality of being friendly, generous, and considerate. A person with kindness gives others their time, effort, and talent when they are in need.

Social Intelligence: The capacity to know oneself and others. A person with social intelligence possesses an awareness of others and the ability to accurately read verbal, non-verbal, and contextual cues. A person with high social intelligence develops from experiences with people and learns from successes and failures in social settings.

Justice: A core virtue that perfects the will; the quality of being fair and reasonable. Comes from the Latin word "Jus," which means "right."

Teamwork: The combined action of a group of people, especially when effective and efficient. A person with the quality of teamwork is socially responsible, loyal, and a team player.

Fairness: Impartial and just treatment or behavior without favoritism or discrimination. A person with fairness is just and doesn't let feelings affect decisions about others.

Leadership: The action of leading a group of people. A person with leadership organizes group activities, encourages the group to get things done, and ensures good relations among group members.

Temperance: The quality of moderation or self-restraint. A person with temperance is disciplined and can self-govern their appetite for pleasure or instant gratification. A core virtue. The Latin root is "temperantia" which means "moderation."

Forgiveness: A conscious decision to release feelings of resentment or vengeance towards yourself or a person or group that has harmed you, regardless of whether they deserve it or not. A person who forgives is merciful, accepts others' shortcomings, and gives people a second chance.

Humility: A modest view of one's own importance: lets their accomplishments speak for themselves and doesn't seek recognition or try to be the center of attention.

Prudence: The quality of being cautious; acts carefully and cautiously to avoid unnecessary risks; makes plans with the future in mind.

Self-Regulation: Governing one's self without intervention from an outside source; managing their own feelings and actions and acts with self-controlled discipline.

Transcendence: Existence or experience beyond the normal or physical level; sees beyond their own personal concerns from a higher perspective and connects to the larger universe to find meaning.

Appreciation of Beauty & Excellence: Noticing the value and beauty of the world, people, and things; recognizing everything around them and emotionally experiencing and appreciating the beauty in the world, people, and the things around them.

Gratitude: The quality of being thankful; readiness to show appreciation for, and to return kindness.

Hope: A feeling of expectation and desire for a certain thing to happen. A person with hope is realistic and also full of optimism about the future, believing in their actions and feeling confident things will turn out well.

Humor: The quality of being amusing or comic, provoking laughter; approaching life playfully, and finding humor in stressful and difficult situations.

Spirituality: The quality of being concerned with the human spirit or soul as opposed to material or physical things; feels a sense of purpose and meaning in life and sees their place in the grand scheme of things. Knows their place in the universe.[12]

"Courage. Kindness. Friendship. Character. These are the qualities that define us as human beings, and propel us, on occasion, to greatness."
– R.J. Palacio, *Wonder*

"Character is determined more by the lack of certain experiences than by those one has had."
– Friedrich Nietzsche

"Good character is not formed in a week or a month. It is created little by little, day by day. Protracted and patient effort is needed to develop good character."
– Heraclitus

"You cannot dream yourself into a character; you must hammer and forge yourself one."
– Henry David Thoreau

<u>KAIZEN</u>

Kaizen is a Japanese business philosophy of continuous improvement of working practices, personal efficiency, etc. The practice of continually improving. It is usually applied to business practices, but can also apply to the self. Work on becoming the best version of yourself every single day. Use the previous lists and your desire to change to re-design yourself into the person you've always wanted to be and never stop improving! Hold yourself to a high standard and hold yourself accountable to becoming the person you want to be.

2¢ Kaizen has become a mantra for me. Whenever I fuck up, whenever I have a loss of control, a temper outburst, unnecessary needless spending, unfairly take my frustrations out on my girlfriend or a loved one, or any of the other countless mistakes I make, I mutter "kaizen" to myself. I realize I have to devote some extra energy and mental capacity to whatever hiccup just occurred and take the proper course of action to prevent if from happening again. Usually this ends up being concentrated effort and meditation.

<u>Self-Worth</u>

Self-worth is the sense of one's own value or worth as a person. In other words, self-worth is a state of being that is defined by self-acceptance, self-respect, self-understanding, and self-love. The most important thing to understand is that self-worth is not based on anything external, it's all about how you feel about yourself.

"A man cannot be comfortable without his own approval."
– Mark Twain

<u>Self-Talk</u>

Self-Talk: The way you talk to yourself about yourself. That little voice in your head. Pay close attention to the narrative there. It's important to keep an upper hand on the small inner battles inside your head every moment of every day. Your thoughts lead to your actions, and your actions are who you are. Successfully catching and correcting your thoughts and self-talk from negative to positive is a giant victory. These small victories add up and contribute to your self-esteem and overall direction in life.

"Your self-talk is the channel of behavior change."
– Gino Norris

Self-Esteem

Self-Esteem: Your opinion of yourself. The way you see, feel, and think about yourself. Your general sense of self-worth. A person with a healthy self-esteem respects themselves and feels they deserve respect from others as well. Conversely, a person with low self-esteem winds up in situations where they aren't proud of themselves, don't respect themselves, and often others don't respect them as well.

"Every new adjustment is a crisis in self-esteem."
– Eric Hoffer

Self-Confidence

Self-Confidence: The way you view your abilities to do certain things. A feeling of trust in one's abilities, qualities, and judgment. Experiencing genuinely positive feelings about yourself while accepting your faults and foibles.

"The way to develop self-confidence is to do the thing you fear and get a record of successful experiences behind you."
-William Jennings Bryan

Putting It All Together

There are entire books written on each of these subjects on how improving them can positively alter your life. Negative self-talk, low self-esteem, and low self-confidence all go hand-in-hand and contribute to overall low self-worth. If you begin to work on and improve your self-talk, it will have compounding benefits that carry over into and improve your self-esteem, self-confidence, and self-worth. If you're not accustomed to healthy and positive self-talk or were in the habit of negative self-talk, then changing to positive self-talk will require a lot of mindfulness and practice.

When you are using positive self-talk, your self-esteem naturally grows. When you are trying something new, your self-confidence builds up over time with repetition. Once you put these all together, you will start believing in yourself, and you will start to have more faith in the process. You will begin to feel hopeful and confident about your future.

Self-talk, self-esteem, and self-worth are prerequisites for building self-confidence. If you have low self-worth but walk around pretending to be confident, it is fake and people will see through it. It is like a pyramid; you must first put in the work to fix your self-esteem and self-worth before you can begin building true self-confidence, which rests at the top of the pyramid. To have true confidence, you must first feel good about yourself and have positive self-talk.

2¢ When I hit the streets, my confidence was at an all-time low. I questioned every thought and move I made. But I had the healthiest and highest sense of self-worth and self-esteem I've ever had. My self-talk was extremely positive and my courage was running high... It allowed me to take those first steps into an MMA gym (being an MMA fighter was my dream career at the time). I knew nothing, but stuck with it and my confidence and skill level grew. The more I tried and learned and improved, the more my confidence grew. I began believing in myself more and more and I kept raising the ceiling on what I thought was possible for me to achieve. It was a snowball effect that continues to this day.

I am David Fucking Goggins. I exist; therefore, I complete what I start. I take pride in my effort and in my performance in all phases of life. Just because I am here! If I'm lost, I will find myself. As long as I'm on planet Earth, I will not half-ass it. Anywhere I lack, I will improve because I exist and I am willing.
-David Goggins

Benefits of Self-Confidence

1. **Being your best under stress.** Athletes, musicians, and actors will attest to the importance of a high level of confidence. When you're confident, you perform up to your potential and you want to perform your best when it counts the most, when under pressure.

2. **Influencing others.** Self-confident people often influence others more readily. This helps when selling an idea or product or negotiating at work or home.

3. **Having leadership and executive presence.** Self-confidence plays a big part in leadership and executive presence. You create such presence by how you think, act (including how you carry your body), and use your voice.

4. **Exuding a more positive attitude.** When you feel confident about yourself, you believe you have an important and meaningful place in the world, giving you a positive attitude.

5. **Feeling valued.** When you're confident, you know what you excel at and that you have value.

6. **Rising to the top.** Looking for a promotion? The more confidence you have, the more likely you are to be promoted.

7. **Being sexier.** Did you know that confidence is sexy? I wrote an article about it, which I published on my website and on YourTango.com. It's one of my most popular articles, and it cracks me up that Google ranks me as number one for the keyword "confidence is sexy."

8. **Reducing negative thoughts.** Greater self-confidence allows you to experience freedom from self-doubt and negative thoughts about yourself.

9. **Experiencing more fearlessness and less anxiety.** Greater confidence makes you more willing to take smart risks and more able to move outside your comfort zone.

10. **Having greater freedom from social anxiety.** Becoming more comfortable being yourself reduces concern about what others might think of you. How liberating!

11. **Gaining energy and motivation to take action.** Confidence gives you positive energy to take action to achieve your personal and professional goals and dreams. The more highly motivated and energized you are, the more likely you are to take immediate action.

12. **Being happier.** Confident people tend to be happier and more satisfied with their lives than people who lack self-confidence.[13]

How to Build Self Confidence

1. **Control your self-talk.** Yes, it's easy to say and hard to do, but you can consciously control some, or most, of your self-talk. Your mind is always listening to your self-talk, and based on this inner talk, it is programming itself like a computer. To be confident, make sure your inner self-talk creates more, not less, self-confidence. Conscious use of affirmations can be helpful.

2. **Change one word.** This can increase your confidence and probability of success when performing under pressure. It's the difference between first and second-person self-talk. First-person self-talk begins with "I." Examples of first-person self-talk include "I've got this!" and "I can do this!" Second-person self-talk begins with "you," or by stating your name. For example, "You've got this!", "You can do this!", "(your name) has got this!", and "(your name) can do this!" The research on this one small change is stunning! A recent research study indicates that this change not only dramatically reduced one's response to stress, but also greatly improved the number of successful outcomes!

3. **Use imagery (visualization).** It surprises most people to learn that they can consciously strengthen confidence much like strengthening a muscle. To strengthen a muscle, you engage it and fire the neurons to make it contract. Each time you do this, the muscle fibers multiply and get larger — you get stronger. Similarly, whenever you think of a time you were confident, you stimulate the neural pathways in your brain where your confident memory resides. Every time these pathways are stimulated, its neurons get thicker and make more dendrite connections. Thus, they get stronger, and your confidence grows. You can learn how to do this by engaging what may be the most powerful self-help technique to build your self-confidence —visualization.

4. **Use routines.** Almost all Olympic and professional athletes use pre-event and pregame routines to help them be their best. Basketball player Kobe Bryant, MVP of the 2009-2010 NBA finals, followed the same routine before every free throw. Three-time Olympic medalist Lindsey Vonn, often referred to as the greatest female American skier in history, creates a clear image in her mind of a perfect run before every race. And in the starting gate, she always clicks her poles together the same way before starting. Why do Olympic and professional athletes work to perfect routines? Because it helps them perform better. Routines can do the same for you.

5. **Give and receive compliments with an open heart.** Strengthening and weakening confidence is complex, yet there's one simple way to build it: learn how to gain confidence by learning how to deeply and fully receive a compliment. Hardly anyone in Western culture fully receives compliments. I catch myself blocking them often, and I teach this stuff. Deflecting compliments runs deep in our culture and starts at a young age.

6. **Prepare obsessively.** Warren Buffett's and Peyton Manning's secret success strategy is the same: they prepare obsessively. I love the juxtaposition of these two men because Peyton Manning is one of the greatest quarterbacks of all time, and Warren Buffet may be the best stock investor ever. Because of their study and preparation, they notice things that other people don't, and they create more opportunities from these observations.

Build your self-confidence with your body.

7. **Be fit or improve your fitness.** In addition to improved mood, happiness, and self-esteem, one of the many benefits of exercise, backed by research, is a boost in self-confidence.
8. **Practice using high-power body positions.** Harvard professor Amy Cuddy's groundbreaking book, "Presence: Bringing Your Boldest Self to Your Biggest Challenges," provides scientific research proving that certain body postures change the hormones that leave you feeling more, or less, powerful and confident.

Minimize your saboteurs.

9. **Learn to stop your negative, destructive thoughts.** Uncontrolled negative thoughts not only hurt your confidence but also your relationships, happiness, and even career. Learn to stop negative, destructive thoughts and build self-confidence with a simple four-step process. I've used this method for three decades; it's powerful if you keep applying it.
10. **Resolve perfectionism.** Are high performers perfectionists? Often, yes. Perfectionism certainly helps you become good or great at what you do. However, perfection is unattainable. The downside is that perfectionistic people are often anxious, and that can lead to depression. It's easy to feel like a failure because you can never achieve perfection.
11. **Choose your tribe carefully.** Negativity is like a highly contagious virus —it's hard not to catch it when you're exposed. Choose to be around positive people who build you and others up. We are all influenced by those around us. Choose your friends, your tribe, carefully!
12. **Master fear in six easy, yet powerful, steps.** Do you have a fear of failure, rejection, or selling? Or other fears that limit your success, relationships, and happiness? Most people do. Irrational fear distorts perception. Imagine wearing red-tinted glasses —everything you see and perceive is red. It's the same with fear. When you look through a lens of fear, things look like you should fear them. You can master the fear of failure, rejection, selling, and other fears![14]

"If we want to fully experience love and belonging, we must believe we are worthy of love and belonging."
– Brene Brown

"Quiet that voice of doubt inside of you. You are good enough. You do deserve good things. You are smart enough. You are worthy of love and respect. You are amazing just the way you are."
– Lorri Faye

"While everyone struggles with occasional dips in self-esteem, those who have chronically low self-esteem may actually be struggling with low self-worth."
– Hailey Shafir, *Self-Worth Vs. Self-Esteem*, 2021

"Mental health issues such as depression or anxiety often come from a lack of self-esteem, lack of worth, lack of acceptance, and struggles to see the positives in yourself."
– Jonny Pardoe, *Self-Esteem and Self-Confidence*, 2019

The Ox & Wagon Metaphor

If you don't like the way you act, change the way you think.

The **Ox** represents the way you think and the **Wagon** represents your actions. The way you think dictates the way you act.

2¢ I don't remember where I first encountered the ox/wagon metaphor but it was midway through my stay in county jail. I began drawing pictures of the Ox/Wagon on my cell walls to remind myself to constantly monitor my thinking. I still love this metaphor and think of it often.

Types of Intelligence

Emotional intelligence (EQ) is defined as the ability to recognize, identify, and manage one's own emotions as well as identify and influence the emotions of others. The point of putting in the work is healing and self-improvement, but a side effect is increased EQ. The deeper you dig into yourself, the higher your EQ can become. So, hold nothing back and leave no stone unturned. Understanding yourself and becoming hyperaware of how you function and operate can also give you better insight into how others function. Increasing your EQ can be super beneficial. With an increased EQ, you can directly confront and work through difficult situations and emotions. This allows you to avoid the negative consequences of not dealing with situations and emotions in the moment. Emotional intelligence allows you to manage stress as it happens and remain calm through chaos.

"Emotional intelligence allows us to respond instead of react."
– Unknown

"Knowing yourself is life's eternal homework."
– Felicia Day

"The most difficult thing in life is to know yourself."
– Thales

"To grow yourself, you must know yourself."
– John C. Maxwell

"Knowing others is wisdom, knowing yourself is enlightenment."
– Lao Tzu

Adversity Quotient AQ – The ability to handle adversities well. "The science of resilience." The term was coined in 1997 by Paul Stoltz in his book Adversity Quotient: Turning Obstacles into Opportunities. The AQ is one of the probable indicators of a person's success in life and is also primarily useful to predict attitude, mental stress, perseverance, longevity, learning, and response to changes in environment. [22]

Your lemonade-making abilities. Your ability to turn a negative into a positive. Your ability to remain positive in the worst situations.

Social Quotient SQ - Social intelligence is the capacity to know oneself and to know others. Social intelligence is learned and developed from experience with people and learning from successes and failures in social settings. Social intelligence is the ability to understand your own and others' actions. It is also known as "tact," "common sense," or "street smarts". It is an important interpersonal skill that helps individuals succeed in all aspects of their lives. [23]

How you fare in social situations. Knowing when to talk and when not to. Being able to "read the room." Knowing how to make people laugh and feel comfortable. Knowing how to connect and engage with people.

Intelligence quotient IQ - A measure of someone's reasoning ability. How well someone can use information and logic to answer questions or make predictions.

While IQ is probably the most popular form of measuring intelligence, it is likely the least important contributor to one's success and happiness.

Situational Awareness SA - The perception of the elements in the environment, (2) comprehension or understanding of the situation, and (3) projection of future status. [24] People with the highest levels of SA can not only perceive the relevant information for their goals and decisions, they can also integrate that information to understand its meaning or significance and project likely or possible future scenarios. These higher levels of SA are critical for proactive decision-making in demanding environments. [25]

Knowing where you are and what is going on around you. Being aware of your surroundings and any present dangers or possible threats. Feeling the energy of any situation you're in.

<u>Healing Never Stops</u>

Self-healing, self-mastery, and putting in the work on yourself can be some of the most beneficial work you ever do in your life. Having good mental health can alter your path in life. It can make you go from constantly struggling and losing the battle, to gaining the upper hand on your mind and thoughts. This can make all the difference and drastically improve your life. The initial act of putting in the work teaches you how to create good mental health, but this is not a "one and done" type of deal. If you want to live a healthy and peaceful life you will have to do regular routine maintenance to stay on top of it. In the future, you might not have to do the exhausting amount of work that you have to do now, but you will have to do less intense sessions of these exercises from time to time to stay healthy.

The healing process is ongoing and never stops.

It's important to continue being mindful of your thinking patterns, and if you catch yourself being negative, go on "high alert," focus your attention on your mental health, and nip that negativity in the bud. An emotional outburst, poor display of emotional control, having negative thoughts or self-talk can all be warning signs that you need to put in some more work. Be honest with yourself, acknowledge that this isn't how you want to be, and divert some energy back into figuring out how to better yourself.

Being "too busy" is never a reasonable excuse to neglect correcting your thoughts and behavior. Fuck excuses. Always take responsibility for your shit and hold yourself to a high standard. If you start getting off the path, always make time to get back on it. There are plenty of tools available to aid in this. You can use group therapy, hit meetings, get one on one counseling, read or listen to relevant books, practice meditation or deep thought, do physical exercise, take the occasional psilocybin micro-dose, or go for a mixture of different practices. Sit quietly, evaluate what's happening, be honest with yourself, and keep your mental health and mindfulness toward your thoughts the top priority.

This work is sacred, holy, and cleansing to the spirit, heart, and mind. If you put all your heart and mind into the healing and self-mastery process, you can transform yourself and your life. Nothing is more satisfying than mastering yourself and being in charge of your destiny.

It is essential to remember that this healing process never ends. Like everything, once you become proficient at it, you won't have to spend as much time and effort on it as you do in the beginning, but it takes time. Learning to control and own your own mind is not easy, comfortable, or quick, but it will greatly improve the quality of your life.

2¢ Every now and again I feel like I'm getting slightly off track, it sends me into high-alert. I never want to get so far off track that I can't find my way back, so when I notice my thinking is negative or self-talk isn't super positive, if my actions don't align with my goals, I know its time to take a little time-out. This usually just means me taking the week-end to sit and be alone with my thoughts, maybe a little psylocibin micro dose along with some meditation and coming up with a plan to get back on track. I always make time for prioritizing my mental health and keeping my mindset positive.

"The soul always knows what to do to heal itself. The challenge is to silence the mind."
– Caroline Myss

"You have the power to heal your life, and you need to know that. We think so often that we are helpless, but we're not. We always have the power of our minds... Claim and consciously use your power."
– Louise L. Hay

"Healing is an art, it takes time, it takes practice, it takes love."
– Maza Dohta

"The idea behind emotional regulation is not to suppress or deny emotions but to manage them consciously as they shape our words and actions."
– Unknown

Part 2 - Plan

Introduction to Planning

Time to shift gears by looking to the future and exercising a different part of your brain. This will be a more enjoyable part of doing time: daydreaming about the shit you're going to do when you're out. Don't let yourself look to the future with gloom, fear, and anxiety. The future is for goals and planning the blueprint for the rest of your life. This is the rebirth. You are the phoenix rising from the ashes; a stronger, wiser, more powerful, and better version of yourself in every way. Look to the future with hope. Have faith that you will eventually succeed if you stay positive and persistent in your quest. Deep down, you may have always had a dream or something extraordinary that you wanted to do with your life. But in the past, doubts, fears, insecurities, and flawed ways of thinking might've held you back. That's all over now. Now things are different. You've re-wired your brain and overhauled your thoughts. You have healthy self-esteem and your self-talk is positive... "Yes I can" type of shit. You've been putting in the work on yourself and it's starting to show. Believing in yourself and feeling hopeful about your future is a powerful thing; it can make all the difference when trying to achieve something. It's time to look to the future and visualize. It's time to dream big.

But what are you going to do? What is your endeavor going to be? This can be a very hard thing to figure out, but chances are you have some sort of dream, some vision you've held onto that can be achieved if you are living to your true potential. Whatever it is, it's not going to be easy. Even with all the proper planning and preparation, things can go wrong, and you will likely be met with resistance at every turn. Are you going to let that stop you? Are you going to let possible failure and humiliation deter you from trying to live out your dreams? Are you going to let the small voice of self-doubt in your head win? Surely, this will lead to "deathbed regret," and if there is one giant motivating factor, it is to not feel regret and sorrow for a life wasted when you reach the end.

This part is focused on utilizing your natural strengths and inclinations... what you're good at, what you enjoy doing, and what you want to do. Maybe there's something you've always wanted to do, but never had the courage to try. This is about mustering up courage, manning the fuck up, and making a pact with yourself to give it a shot. Thinking it through far and wide and creating a plan of action to make it happen. This can be a fun part of doing time, getting lost in the daydream, but try to keep it practical and focused. It's okay to be lofty, but always remember, there will come a day when you gotta step up and take action to make these things happen. Use this time to visualize what you will have to do. Think about the roadblocks and resistance you will encounter, think of the difficulties you are going to face, and the toughness and resilience it is going to take to see it through. This is a valuable time to use for meditating on just how deep you are going to have to dig.

"A goal without a plan is just a wish."
– Antoine de Saint-Exupéry

"By failing to prepare, you are preparing to fail."
– Benjamin Franklin

Andrew Carnegie - The Path from Poverty to Riches

Andrew Carnegie was a Scottish-American industrialist and philanthropist. Carnegie led the expansion of the American steel industry in the late 19th century and became one of the richest Americans in history. He became a leading philanthropist in the United States, Great Britain, and the British Empire. During the last 18 years of his life, he gave away around $350 million (roughly $5.5 billion in 2021) to charities, foundations, and universities. This was almost 90 percent of his fortune.[15]

I want to share one of my favorite passages from "How to Own your Own Mind" by Napoleon Hill where the author interviews Carnegie. The interview took place in the late 1800's so it's a little outdated, but the message is timeless and elegant:

"I've always been interested in understanding more about the transition by which one changes from poverty to riches. Practically every man of great wealth in the United States appears to have started from scratch with nothing but a sound mind and an opportunity such as every man has under the American way of life..."

"...the man who prepares himself to change from poverty to riches is something like a farmer who wishes to convert a forest into a productive field; he first clears away the timber and debris, then he plows the ground and conditions the soil, after that he plants the seed, but all these steps have to be taken intelligently and at the right season of the year or no crop will be realized. It is precisely the same procedure with the man who makes up his mind to be done with poverty; he must first clear his mind of all negative and self-imposed limitations, then he must take inventory of his education, experience, natural aptitudes, and general ability to see what he has to offer. After this he must look for a market for whatever service he is capable of rendering. Here enters one of the more important of the principles of individual achievement: the principle of going the extra mile. I have never heard of anyone changing from poverty to riches without applying this principle and doing it as a matter of habit. Up to this point the preparation has consisted mainly of the clearing away of the obstacles that stand between men and success. The next step is that of making oneself success conscious; riches have a way of gravitating toward the man who has made up his mind to have them. Indolence, indifference, self-imposed limitations, fear, and discouragement will never attract riches. After a man has attracted favorable attention to himself by the habit of going the extra mile, he

is then in a position to adopt a definite major purpose and to begin expressing it in action through a definite plan. His major purpose naturally will be based upon the sort of service he has for sale. From this point on he applies the principles of individual achievement in whatever combinations and under whatever circumstances his major purpose requires, but mind you, he does not quit when the going becomes hard, if he has properly charged his mind with success consciousness he will not want to quit. This preparation is an absolute essential for the acquisition of riches. Here let me offer the warning that the man whose only object is to acquire riches will more than likely meet with disappointment. The best of all mental attitudes in which to begin the transition from poverty to riches is that in which a man center's his thoughts more upon the surface he renders than on the riches he is seeking. Riches which are sought merely for the sake of the riches alone have many forms of evasiveness by which they avoid capture. Alas, I fear there are too few who recognize this truth. I sincerely believe that the best way for a man to accumulate riches is by making himself indispensable through some form of useful service, all my experience confirms this. All that I have learned from the experiences of other men supports this thought."

-Andrew Carnegie[16]

"the man who prepares himself to change from poverty to riches is something like a farmer who wishes to convert a forest into a productive field; he first clears away the timber and debris, then he plows the ground and conditions the soil, after that he plants the seed, but all these steps have to be taken intelligently and at the right season of the year or no crop will be realized."

-Andrew Carnegie

Dreams

Dream: A cherished aspiration, ambition, or ideal. A vision created in the imagination.

You've probably always had a dream, but never taken it seriously or believed in yourself enough to go after it. That all changes now. Now, you are going to be the person that goes for it. The person that overcomes the fear, that silences the inner critic saying "You can't do it." The dream you've been holding onto all your life but up until now haven't had the courage to chase. What if you don't have a specific dream, or don't know what you want to do with your life? That's something you have to figure out using your natural strengths and inclinations, more than likely it's something that terrifies you. Maybe you just want to live a normal, mundane life. Well, that's okay too. Even so, there is probably something you want to do with your life, some sort of purpose you feel deep down. It doesn't have to be grandiose or extraordinary, but it will require facing fear, having courage, and getting outside of your comfort zone.

"The one goal that is most important to you at the moment. It is usually the one goal that will help you to achieve more of your other goals than anything else you can accomplish."
– Brian Tracy "Goals"

"Everybody has a dream, but not everybody has a grind."
– Eric Thomas

"Without leaps of imagination or dreaming, we lose the excitement of possibilities. Dreaming, after all, is a form of planning."
– Gloria Steinem

Inclination: A person's natural tendency or urge to act or feel in a particular way; a disposition or propensity.

Your natural gifts and strengths. Things you've always been naturally good at or skills you have built up over time. Your hidden or obvious talents. Something you can do easily that others might struggle with. They can be tangible and physical, like athleticism, hand-eye coordination, and so on. Or they can be intangible, like being able to make people laugh, being able to make others feel comfortable, public speaking, being good at math, or being good with numbers. The list goes on and on. Use your natural inclinations, strengths, and things you're good at and passionate about to help you decide your major purpose in life. Following your purpose day in and day out and never giving up puts you on the path of chasing your dreams.

2¢ *After the healing work and memento mori epiphany I realized that what really mattered to me is that I just try and go all-in on something. My dream is to take a big shot at something and succeed. With that would come the money and freedom of time, ability to build my own home, start a family and help people.*

"Know what your strengths are and take advantage of them."
– Greg Norman

"So many people think that they are not gifted because they don't have an obvious talent that people can recognize because it doesn't fall under the creative arts category —writing, dancing, music, acting, art, or singing. Sadly, they let their real talents go undeveloped, while they chase after fame. I am grateful for the people with obscure unremarked talents because they make our lives easier —inventors, organizers, planners, peacemakers, communicators, activists, scientists, and so forth. However, there is one gift that trumps all other talents —being an excellent parent. If you can successfully raise a child in this day and age to have integrity then you have left a legacy that future generations will benefit from."
– Shannon L. Alder

Definite Major Purpose

The thing that you decide to do with your life. Your purpose. If your dream is to "be rich," then how you will get rich is your purpose. The means by which you achieve your dreams. This is probably one of the hardest things to figure out. It can also be very easy to know, but difficult to admit to. One thing is certain, no one can choose this for you. Once you have decided your purpose, you must create a plan to get there and find the courage to take action. If you want to be a famous rapper with foreign cars then you gotta have a beat and start spittin' bars.

What you'll have to do will likely include activities that cause resistance. In his book "The War of Art," Steven Pressfield lists several activities that most commonly produce resistance:

1) The pursuit of any creative calling: writing, painting, music, film, dance, or any other art, however marginal or unconventional.

2) The launching of any entrepreneurial venture or enterprise for profit or otherwise.

3) Any diet or health regimen.

4) Any program of spiritual advancement.

5) Any activity whose aim is tighter abdominals.

6) Any course or program designed to overcome an unwholesome habit or addiction.

7) Education of every kind.

8) Any act of political, moral, or ethical courage. Including the decision to change oneself for the better by changing one's patterns of thought and action.

9) The undertaking of any enterprise or endeavor whose aim is to help others.

10) Any act that entails commitment of the heart. Examples are the decision to get married, have a child, or weather a rocky patch in a relationship.

11) The taking of a principled stance in the face of adversity. In other words, any act that rejects immediate gratification in favor of long-term growth, health, or integrity. Expressed differently, any action that derives from our higher nature instead of our lower.[17]

"Desire is the factor that determines what your definite purpose in life shall be. No one can select your dominating desire for you, but once you select it yourself, it becomes your definite chief aim and occupies the spotlight of your mind until it is satisfied by transformation into reality, unless you permit it to be pushed aside by conflicting desires... these are the steps leading from desire to fulfillment: first the burning desire, then the crystallization of that desire into a definite purpose. Then sufficient appropriate action to achieve that purpose. Remember that these three steps are always necessary to ensure success."

– Napoleon Hill

"All successful people, men and women, are big dreamers. They imagine what their future could be, ideal in every respect, and then they work every day toward their distant vision, that goal or purpose."

– Brian Tracy

"Nothing in this world is worth having or worth doing unless it means effort, pain, difficulty. No kind of life is worth leading if it is always an easy life. I know that your life is hard; I know that your work is hard; and hardest of all for those of you who have the highest trained consciences, and who therefore feel always how much you ought to do. I know your work is hard, and that is why I congratulate you with all my heart. I have never in my life envied a human being who led an easy life; I have envied a great many people who led difficult lives and led them well."
– Theodore Roosevelt

"I will leverage my strengths, mitigate my weaknesses, and achieve my goals."
– Brandon Morelock

"I hope that you scrape every dollar you can, I hope you know money won't erase the pain."
– J. Cole, MIDDLE CHILD

Reverse Engineering and Setting Goals

Reverse Engineering: deconstructing individual components of a larger product to see how it is made and works.

The last chapter brought up what is arguably the most difficult part of the process: deciding what you want to do with your life. What is your definite major purpose? What will your legacy be? You must decide and you must commit to it fully. Use your ability to visualize and daydream the ideal life you want for yourself in 5, 10, 20 years. Then, you simply reverse-engineer it. Work your way backward from that 20-year vision of your ideal life all the way back to you sitting right there in that cell. This is how you come up with sets and subsets of goals that all fit into and stack on top of each other. That 20-year vision you dream up in the cell may not occur, but if you give it a try, a real effort, it will set you on a course that ends up being a purpose-driven life… not to be all cliché, but it's about the journey. It can always change and evolve along the way, but the important thing is having a start-ing point and giving it a significant effort. If you don't end up actually reach-ing your goal, but you really gave it a go, you will at least not be saying "what if."

Reverse engineering your dream: using the power of visualization, start at the endpoint of your ideal life (that moment where you're congratulating yourself saying, "I did it"). Press rewind from that point, and there will be major events that lead back to where you are currently. The time leading up to the endpoint will be very unclear. But when you get to 1 month out, 3 months out, 6 months out, and 1 year out, you can start listing a tangible set of goals for yourself.

2¢ Getting out, my goal was to be an MMA fighter. It started with me joining an MMA gym within the first week of getting out. Within two weeks of getting out, I got a job for income. Then the next goal was to learn Jiu-Jitsu and Muay Thai. I wanted to get my BJJ blue belt in nine months (unrealistic). I planned to have my first fight within twelve months of starting. Of course, injuries happened in training and set me back, but I had a series of goals with one leading up to the next.

Reverse Engineering Your Dream Process

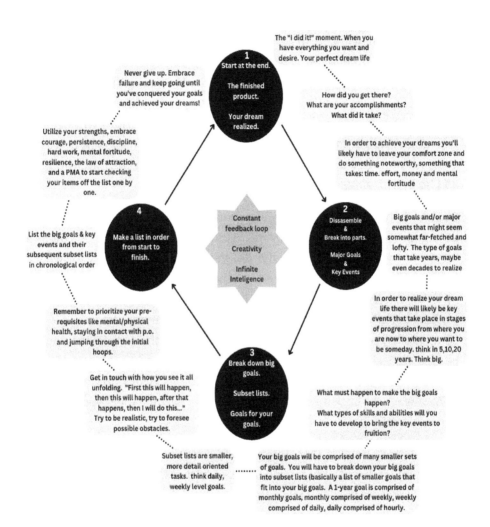

Goals

Goal: The object of a person's ambition or effort; an aim or desired result. When you're setting goals; think on an hourly, daily, weekly, monthly, and yearly basis, then try to make them all fit inside each other. A series of hourly goals will help you achieve your daily goals, a series of daily goals will help you achieve your weekly goals, weekly goals contribute to your monthly goals and monthly goals fit into your yearly goals. Never go to bed without thinking about your goals for the upcoming day. Start writing down your goals and getting in the habit of checking them off. Looking at a list of goals with lots of check marks is a great way to keep track of your progress and hold yourself accountable.

Goals provide a starting point and actionable steps. Don't be afraid to set lofty goals and fail. Don't let failures discourage you, instead, use them as feedback for making adjustments. Relish the failure and see it for what it really is: a learning experience and a chance to grow. "There's no such thing as failures, only learning experiences." Be excited for your first "learning experience." Be excited to get out there and chase your dreams, but also be mentally prepared to fail. Always remember, with every failure you will be one step closer to victory. You can use the failures to reevaluate and recalculate your path. Ultimately, failures serve as guides on your journey. If you always get back up and try again, failures become the stepping stones and guide rails of your winding journey.

What matters most is that you try. Use lists; write down your goals and hang them up. Constantly remind yourself of them; stare at them, and hold yourself accountable to tackle them. Make daily, weekly, monthly, and yearly lists. If you let life get in the way your goals can hit the backburner. The time is now to make the decision to never let that happen and reinforce yourself with that "never give up" attitude.

Dream board. A dream board is where you compile your goals, motivations, and aspirations using quotes, pictures, and anything visual that you can look at daily that will remind you of your dreams, why you have these particular goals, and what you want to do with your life. Use visual aids to help motivate and keep the fire burning in you.

2¢ I drew a picture of my dream house and I visualized myself 20 years out, thanking myself in jail for doing this work, making these goals, and going for them. I used a mixture of pictures and words for my dream board because I'm terrible at drawing. My dream board consisted of me being a champion MMA fighter, building my dream house, a nice car, money, a family with dogs and cats, buying my mom, dad, and brother a house, authoring a book, and speaking in front of or entertaining crowds of people.)

"One should not pursue goals that are easily achieved. One must develop an instinct for what one can just barely achieve through one's greatest efforts."
– Albert Einstein

"You are never too old to set another goal or dream a new dream."
– Les Brown

"A goal is a dream with a deadline."
– Napoleon Hill
"Set your mind on a definite goal and observe how quickly the world stands aside to let you pass"
– Napoleon Hill

Visualize, Mentally Prepare, and CBT

Visualize: To form a mental image of something.

Mentally prepare: Preparing your mind for a future situation in your life.

When it comes to success and reaching your potential, start visualizing the type of life you want to live, and the kind of person you want to be. What does your ideal life look like? Do you want to have the log mansion on the lake with the Range Rover in the driveway? It's not just going to get handed to you. It's going to take years and years of grinding it out and hard fucking work to get there. You're going to get out and be starting from scratch. There are going to be countless obstacles and setbacks. You're going to have to start from the very bottom, the mud, the trenches, and dig your way out, thought by thought, minute by minute, step by step, day by day. You're going to have some tough fucking days ahead of you, you're going to have to dig deep to get there. This is going to require discipline, patience, persistence, and a positive mental attitude. You'll be hit with fear and doubt, and your insecurities are going to resurface. Resistance is going to hit you from every angle. Are you going to let it win, or will you master your thoughts and conquer that shit? Don't wait until you're faced with it to find out, try looking into the future and visualize the win. Start meditating and imagining what it's going to take to get there. It's going to take everything you've got. Physically it is going to take time, money, blood, sweat, and tears. Mentally it will require a deep burning desire, discipline, persistence, sacrifice, faith, patience, hard work, and staying positive in the face of adversity and setbacks.

2¢ *I remember seeing Lebron James cry after he got his 3rd ring, the way he just fell to the ground, crying like a little baby, "I did it." I've always wanted that "I did it" moment. I have burnt into my mind reaching that "I did it" moment, the details like when, where, or how it happens are blurry, but the emotions I will feel and the tears running down my face are a crystal-clear image. I use that visual to motivate me. "Can't stop 'til I cry like Lebron." There are a few events that could make me cry like that… becoming a millionaire, buying my mom a house, marrying a good woman and having a kid. I visualize making these things happen. None of them have happened yet, but I have such strong faith that they will. I continue using visualization… the more feedback I get the more detailed the visualizing and goal setting becomes. I am highly motivated to make these things happen, so they will. Simple as that. I will not stop until they do.*

When it comes to relapse and using drugs, chances are you've got a pretty good idea of what types of situations make you most vulnerable. A good way to ensure that you can see your way through tough and triggering situations once you're out is to start mentally preparing for them now. Just saying no is easier said than done. Visualize yourself encountering a peer-pressure moment or relapse from your past and successfully navigating through it. Visualize the win, think about how hard it is to pass up, and all the little tricks your mind plays in those moments. Think about how good it will feel to say no, think about how much progress will be lost if you say yes, think about that 20-year vision of your dream life and that it'll never happen if you go down the drug path again. Identify the types of high-risk situations you will want to avoid, but be prepared for how to handle them if you do happen to find yourself in one. Are you going to be stable enough to remain true to your positive self when the times get tough?

Premeditatio Malorum: The premeditation of the evils and troubles that might lie ahead. It's the exercise of imagining things that could go wrong or be taken away from us. It helps us prepare for life's inevitable setbacks. We don't always get what is rightfully ours, even if we've earned it. Not everything is as clean and straightforward as we think it should be. Psychologically, we must prepare ourselves for this to happen.

Cognitive Behavioral Therapy

Cognitive behavioral therapy (CBT): a common type of talk therapy, psychotherapy. CBT helps you become aware of inaccurate or negative thinking so you can view challenging situations more clearly and respond to them more effectively.[18] Either alone or in combination with other types of therapy, CBT can be a very helpful tool for treating mental health disorders such as depression, post-traumatic stress disorder (PTSD), drug addiction, or an eating disorder. But not everyone who benefits from CBT has a mental health condition. CBT can be an effective tool to help anyone learn how to better manage stressful life situations.

"Rehearse them in your mind: exile, torture, war, shipwreck. All the terms of our human lot should be before our eyes."
– Seneca

Create a Mission Statement

Mission Statement: a formal summary of the aims and values of a company, organization, or individual.

The three components of a mission statement include the purpose, values, and goals of an entity. In this case, it's just a sentence or two that sums up your overarching theme or goal. A mission statement broadly states your mission in life. It can be used on a dream board or as something you recite to yourself to remind you of your "what" and "why."

2¢ Shortly after reading "The 7 Habits of Highly Effective People," I rented a cabin in the woods solely for the purpose of getting away and coming up with my mission statement. It's vague but captures the essence of what I've been trying to do with my life since deciding I wanted to be an extraordinary individual. I still have it written on my whiteboard and I still recite it to myself occasionally.

"To set lofty goals and achieve them while being a multi-faceted force for good."

Make a Pact with Yourself

Pact: A formal agreement between individuals or parties.

This is a tool to help keep you motivated and accountable to yourself. It can be a sacred promise you make to yourself to go all in on life and never give up. Making a serious pact with yourself can strengthen you when fear and doubt creep in.

Make a pact with yourself that you will take the first step toward achieving your goals. Don't focus too much on the end product of your vision because it may change along the way. Instead, focus your pact more on something like always being courageous or always stepping outside your comfort zone. Make a pact to always choose courage over fear. Make a pact to keep getting back up if you fall and never give up no matter what. Make a pact to stay positive and not say "fuck it" and go back to getting high. Make a pact that will trudge you through your lows. Make a pact to always be disciplined and do what you know you should be doing, even when you don't feel like doing so. And make a pact not to do what you know you shouldn't do, even when you want to do so. Make a pact to try and achieve your own personal greatness, whatever that may be. Make a pact to not feel regret at the end of your life.

2¢ I have fallen back on the pacts I made with myself while I was in there many times. In the toughest moments when I'm feeling hopeless and negative thoughts start creeping in, I remember the deal I made with myself and I draw strength from it. My pact was to constantly be outside of my comfort zone and take business risks. Just recently I was mentally stuck on making the first big purchase order for my latest fitness product… I remembered the pact I made with myself, and I pulled the trigger. I'm so glad I made that pact with myself because it has always helped me to snap out of fearful and negative thinking. And I'm also proud of myself for always holding myself accountable to it.

"When you make an agreement and you don't keep it you undermine your own self trust."

– Roy Baumeister

Courage (again)

Courage: Courage is the ability to face and overcome fear, danger, pain, or adversity. It is a quality that allows individuals to act despite risks or uncertainty. Courage is not the absence of fear but rather the willingness to confront it and move forward in the face of it. It often involves taking a difficult or unpopular stand, speaking up for what is right, or facing difficult challenges. Courage can be demonstrated in different ways, from physical acts of bravery to standing up for one's beliefs and values, and it is a highly valued trait in many cultures and societies.

Courage is knowing you could fail, feeling fear, and going for it anyway. Courage is going against the grain. Courage is making your own path. Courage is doing the right thing when everyone else is doing the wrong thing.

"Courage…There is nothing we prize more, but find shorter in supply."

-Unknown

Mustering Courage & Accountability

Muster: to assemble, especially for inspection or in preparation for battle; to produce or encourage something such as an emotion or support.

While you sit in your cell, walk the pod/yard, do your pushups, lay in your bunk and stare at the ceiling, every moment you spend locked up…

...MUSTER COURAGE NON-STOP, RELENTLESSLY.

Begin fortifying your courage to act on your goals when you get out. It's easy to sit there daydreaming and planning, but following through is hard. You'll need lots of courage when you get out, so start loading up on it now. Think of this time as charging up. You're locked up, but you're plugged in; charging your courage like a cell phone plugged into a charger. You came in broken, but if you use this time to put in work and muster the courage, you'll come out with a purpose and a plan. And when the time comes, you'll be fully charged to overcome anything that gets in the way of you and your goals. Fuck fear. Fuck doubt. Fuck excuses. Fuck anyone and anything that gets in between you and your goals and dreams.

Accountability: An obligation or willingness to accept responsibility or to account for one's actions.

Accountability partner: An accountability partner is someone who supports another person to keep a commitment or maintain progress on a desired goal. Usually a trusted friend or acquaintance who will regularly ask you about your progress.

Become your own accountability partner. No one else is going to achieve your goals for you. No one is going to fully see the vision for your life, and no one is going to believe in you. You're going to have to believe in yourself and your vision before anyone else starts to. Start becoming self-reliant in there so you can be self-reliant when you hit the streets.

Exercise and a Healthy Routine

The benefits of exercise are plentiful:

Help you control your weight. Along with diet, exercise plays an important role in controlling your weight and preventing obesity. To maintain your weight, the calories you eat and drink must equal the energy you burn. To lose weight, you must use more calories than you eat and drink.

Reduce your risk of heart disease. Exercise strengthens your heart and improves your circulation; the increased blood flow raises the oxygen levels in your body. This helps lower your risk of heart diseases such as high cholesterol, coronary artery disease, and heart attack. Regular exercise can also lower your blood pressure and triglyceride levels.

Help your body manage blood sugar and insulin levels. Exercise can lower your blood sugar level and help your insulin work better. This can cut down your risk for metabolic syndrome and type 2 diabetes. And if you already have one of those, exercise can help you to manage it.

Help you quit smoking. Exercise may make it easier to quit smoking by reducing your cravings and withdrawal symptoms. It can also help limit the weight you might gain when you stop smoking.

Improve your mental health and mood. During exercise, your body releases chemicals that can improve your mood and make you feel more relaxed. This can help you deal with stress and reduce your risk of depression.

Help keep your thinking, learning, and judgment skills sharp as you age. Exercise stimulates your body to release proteins and other chemicals that improve the structure and function of your brain.

Strengthen your bones and muscles. Regular exercise can help kids and teens build strong bones. Later in life, it can also slow the loss of bone density that comes with age. Doing muscle-strengthening activities can help you increase or maintain your muscle mass and strength.

Reduce your risk of cancers. Exercise can reduce your risk of developing many cancers including colon, breast, uterine, and lung cancer.

Reduce your risk of falls. For older adults, research shows that doing balance and muscle-strengthening activities in addition to moderate-intensity aerobic activity can help reduce your risk of falling.

Improve your sleep. Exercise can help you to fall asleep faster and stay asleep longer.

Improve your sexual health. Regular exercise may lower the risk of erectile dysfunction (ED) in men. For those who already have ED, exercise may help improve their sexual function. In women, exercise may increase sexual arousal.

Increase your chances of living longer. Studies show that physical activity can reduce your risk of dying early from the leading causes of death, like heart disease and some cancers. [19]

Ameliorate your Stress. Try ameliorating stressful moments and eliminating mental anguish by processing information during an intense physical workout. Get your heart rate up in a high zone and keep it up while you're thinking and processing tough or stressful information. This can get you in the habit of using exercise to de-stress, process, decompress, and cope with situations in a healthy manner. Exercise can also be used to release some of the trapped emotions you might have. You can come out of an exercise feeling accomplished, having contributed to your physical and mental health. There's an enormous amount of science backing this up. This can become the centerpiece of your daily routine, a healthy addiction that you can build your day around, and you can take this healthy addiction with you after you get out as well. Make exercise a keystone habit, one that you keep for the rest of your life. (**Ameliorate**: To make something bad or unsatisfactory better. To make better or improve.
Stress: Great worry caused by a difficult situation, or something that causes this situation.)

Exercise builds more than just muscle. It builds character, discipline, self-esteem, and confidence. It gives you goals to work toward. It is one of the greatest things you can do for yourself, and it can add longevity to your life. What are you going to do... lay around and get fat from starchy prison food? Fuck that. Start exercising, it makes doing time so much easier.

Exercise is a great way to build and develop discipline. Discipline is one of the main traits any successful person has. On days that you just don't want to, pushing yourself to do it anyway can give a great boost in mood and pull you out of a rut. Also, having the discipline to keep the exercise routine after being released can be a great way to build a healthy routine on the streets. It can be the pillar of your world when starting over. It helps create healthy momentum in the early days, and it can and will always be a healthy addiction.

Exercise to failure, and in those moments where you're at complete exhaustion, visualize the glory that is to come your way if you achieve your goals and realize your dream. Push your body to its edge and visualize a successful future in those moments, like the moment a little kid has before blowing out the candles on a birthday cake. Burn it into your heart and soul that you will achieve your own personal greatness. At the end of that last rep, think about what you really desire most in life, think about your dreams and the moment you achieve them. Then think about how the only way this will ever happen is if you dig deep and give it all you got, with all your heart and mind, and soul. Think about getting out and having the courage to follow through. Work out as hard as you possibly can (without destroying your joints) and think about success and glory and what motivates you while doing it.

2¢ *I exercised a lot in prison. I pushed myself hard, to failure. And in that moment when I felt like I had nothing left, I would close my eyes and think of all the struggle and pain I'd been through and it gave me a boost to push it harder. I still remember those workouts, that feeling of digging deep. I have continued to exercise, it became the foundation of my post-prison life and I've made it my livelihood (inventing fitness products). Fitness in one form or another has saved my life.*

Exercise became the one constant thing in my life.

"It is a disgrace to grow old through sheer carelessness before seeing what manner of man you may become by developing your bodily strength and beauty to their highest limit."

– Socrates

"Dopamine drives all human behavior... that's a neurotransmitter in your brain that literally affects every single decision that you make... a lot of people like to get their dopamine from alcohol, that's probably gonna ruin your relationships, your friendships and you're probably gonna become an alcoholic. A lot of people like geting dopamine from doing drugs... that's gonna have a negative effect on your life as well... you're probably gonna become a junkie. A lot of people like their dopamine from eating shit food... you're gonna pay for that by becoming an unhealthy person. A lot of people like getting their dopamine from vigorous, intense exercise like me... you're gonna pay for that by hard work and sweat. How are you gonna get your dopamine?"

– Tanner Shuck

Check out the exercise routines starting on page 127 from Jailhouse Strong

The Plan Is Always Evolving

As your release comes closer and closer, it is essential to have pre-determined first steps. These will be the first actions you take in your first days, weeks, and months of freedom. Choose and act wisely. Before you go to sleep, take a moment to prioritize the coming day and make sure that everything lines up and is true to the vision of the person you want to be and the life you want to live. See the desired outcome of the coming day and know what you're going to have to do in order to live that way. The plan is always evolving, but the most important thing is taking action and following through, no matter the outcome.

The road is going to be a winding one, and chances are that your vision of the future is not going to line up perfectly with your actual path. Still, if you act courageously and commit to going after your dreams, you are guaranteed to live a more fulfilling and purposeful life. It's important to remember life is a roller coaster full of ups and downs. Be sure to take note of and enjoy the highs when they come, and stay positive and learn from the lows when you are experiencing those too.

Remember: "This too shall pass." The lows never last, and neither do the highs. Never be afraid or too busy to take a step back and check your inner compass. Have faith, take a leap, and go after your dreams. Don't sit back and stay comfortable and let fear, doubt or your ego shield you from taking chances and risks. You *can* do it. But you've got to try to DO IT first!

2¢ This is huge. To have a starting point but be willing to re-assess and change course and roll with it. My initial MMA dream evolved into something else at about the 12 month point. I realized I was creative, intelligent and gritty enough to invent a product, start a business around it, market it and sell it. My confidence kept growing, soon my plan evolved to not only be a founder, but a serial founder and serial entrepreneur. Soon I had a 10 year plan that included 4-5 products, multiple books, a podcast, and even producing music. I love the way my post-prison journey has been unfolding and evolving constantly.

"...when we embrace the unexpected... we commonly find ourselves discovering far more, than when we rigidly stick to the original plan. What's more, those unexpected adventures or detours... that we experience... then frequently become, the highlights, memories, or even... meaningful important lessons in life, that we'll forever cherish!"
– AshRawArt

"Most of all, do not be too quick to denounce your sufferings. The difficult road you are called to walk may, in fact, be your only path to success."
– Richard Paul Evans, *A Winter Dream*

"Life has a tendency to provide a person with what they need in order to grow. Our beliefs, what we value in life, provide the roadmap for the type of life that we experience. A period of personal unhappiness reveals that our values are misplaced and we are on the wrong path. Unless a person changes their values and ideas, they will continue to experience discontentment."
– Kilroy J. Oldster, *Dead Toad Scrolls*

"When defeat comes, accept it as a signal your plans are not sound, rebuild those plans and set sail once more toward your coveted goal."
– Napoleon Hill

Part 3 - Execute

Getting Out and Taking Action

The daydreaming comes to an end. Countless hours of thought have been spent on this very moment and the ensuing days. You're getting out. Better, stronger, wiser. A person with a plan. Take slow calculated steps; adopt a slow sustainable rise with a solid foundation over a quick rise built on sand. It takes enormous courage to take the first step in a new direction. Don't get hellbent on perfection as you're taking those first steps. The most important thing is that you show up and try. There's always going to be time to regroup and change the plan as needed, but for now, the most important thing is to start somewhere. The main theme is 'taking action', doing something, and going for it. Getting outside of your comfort zone and taking calculated risks. Of course, you don't want to fail, but it's a necessary part of the process. Try to view failure as something good, yearn for it. Every failure is one step closer to victory. Get a couple of fails under your belt and you begin to see that it really isn't that bad. Each time you learn massively, you can recalibrate, regroup, and come back better every time.

There will inevitably be things that get in the way, hoops you must jump through that end up putting your plans and goals on the back burner. Do what you must, then get back to it. Don't let the dream fade and die, keep the burning desire and feed the flames with small victories and completed objectives.

Setbacks are going to occur, remember that with each setback there is a hidden opportunity, you just have to learn to see it and use it.

Resistance in the form of self-doubt and fear are going to try and put you back in your comfort zone. Be prepared for these things to arise and dim your fire, but don't let them, it's a trick played by the ego to shield you. Don't fall for it. Squash negative thoughts immediately. Stay on top of your thoughts and feelings, and your actions will follow.

You have to take action. You have got to take the first steps. You've got to try. Taking uncomfortable first steps is always hard, but it gets easier and more natural the more you do it, so do it. Harness that neuroplasticity and become a person who goes out there and does shit. Give a genuine effort. If you undertake an endeavor that is out of reach, you will grow and learn so much through it. Become an agent of action.

Try > fail > learn > recalibrate. Try > fail > learn > recalibrate. Try > fail > learn… repeat.

Notice that fear is one of the key elements of this process. Of course, you never try to fail at something, but you'd be wise to accept that it's part of the process so you are mentally prepared to deal with it. Whatever you do, don't get discouraged and quit. Take a moment to acknowledge the pain from a failure, but the best thing you can do is to get over it quickly and snap back into positive mode. Think about what happened and what you can learn from it. See if there's a way you can spin it into something beneficial, come up with a revised plan, and fuckin get back up and try again. You'll be one loss closer to victory.

Do a little bit each day to build momentum and advance your goals. You aren't going to achieve it all in a day, week, or month. It will likely take years. Build strong habits and develop discipline to consistently do a little bit each day, it adds up and soon you'll be a powerhouse juggernaut. Persistent hard work will eventually pay off. Someday, to the onlooker, it will seem like a case of overnight success, but really, it's the culmination of years of healing, planning, and executing on a daily basis. This is the way.

Use memento mori, remember you are going to die, YOLO baby. Fucking go for it.

2¢ I spent so much time thinking about what I was going to do when I got out, HUGE plans. Lofty plans. I spoke about it only to two people while I was in there. I chose very carefully who I told what my plans were because at that point I couldn't act on them so telling someone opened me up to ridicule and humiliation, and my plans were so lofty that it was almost impossible not to laugh at them. In fact, the people I told did laugh, but they were positive enough to say something like "nothing's impossible, you should go for it." I spent a lot of time wondering if I suffer from delusions of grandeur, and if I'm crazy for thinking I could do what I planned and dreamt up. I would always circle back and answer the question: "am I crazy?" with " there's only one way to find out." And the only way to find out is to try. Two years out I was still wondering if I suffer from delusional thinking, but I do remember a couple specific moments where I almost broke down in tears, I remember I was driving my 98' Ford Ranger and I looked in the rear-view mirror and screamed to myself "IT"S HAPPENING!! IT'S FUCKIN' HAPPEN-ING!!!" I would fall back on the pact I made with myself in there and think what a fuckin waste it would be to do all that planning, and mustering and not even try. I just couldn't live with myself, I couldn't bare it, the only way to have self-respect or self-love was to try. Not trying was not an option anymore. I used to smoke heroin to cope with the self-hatred I accumulated from never trying anything, from always staying safe in the comfort zone. What a thrill it is to try, to go all-in!

"Vision without execution is just hallucination."
– Henry Ford

"Innovation is rewarded. Execution is worshipped."
– Eric Thomas

"Execution is the ability to mesh strategy with reality, align people with goals, and achieve the promised results."
– Lawrence Bossidy

"Very often, a good decision executed quickly beats a brilliant decision implemented slowly or poorly."
– Marcia W. Blenko

"Average people have great ideas. Legends have great execution."
– Anonymous

"In the end, a vision without the ability to execute it is probably a hallucination."
– Steve Case
"Success doesn't necessarily come from breakthrough innovation, but from flawless execution."
– Naveen Jain

"A good plan, violently executed now is better than a perfect plan tomorrow."
– George Patton

"Ideas are cheap. Ideas are easy. Ideas are common. Everybody has ideas. Ideas are highly, highly overvalued. Execution is all that matters."
– Casey Neistat

"Don't just think. Don't just talk. Don't just dream. None of that matters. The only thing that matters is that you actually do. So: DO."
– Jocko Willink

Get Out and Let Good In

Phone # rule – Don't ever give your phone number out to someone who will call you with some bullshit. If you make it a rule to not give your number out except to people who will help you achieve your goals or bring positivity to your life, then you can be excited every time your phone rings. This might mean that you don't get many calls or texts at first. Try to be okay with that. It's going to take a little time before you build a network of positivity in your life.

DON'T GIVE ANYONE YOUR NUMBER THAT WILL BRING NEGATIVITY INTO YOUR LIFE.

This rule can extend beyond your phone to your life as well. Make it a rule to only let good and positive people into your life, into your circle. You probably lost a lot when you got locked up, but chances are a lot of what you lost was good riddance. Don't be in a hurry to flood your life with negative people and connections. In your heart, you know what's good for you and what isn't. And there's a pretty standard rule: who you associate with and what you surround yourself with plays a massive role in who you are. You may have to go it alone for a while, but follow this rule and soon you will find yourself surrounded by positive people with your best interests at heart. Be very selective about who you choose to let back into your life from your past, and if they aren't going to be a positive force in your life, then don't let them in. Don't slide back into that fucking bullshit street life that put you in this place. Be okay with just having your goals to hold onto at first. As you soldier your way through your new life, people will become attracted to your positive energy and you will attract positivity into your life.

2¢ This was one of the first chapters I thought of when this book was conceived. The phone number rule. So important and so simple. Good for anyone in life, not just ex-cons coming out of prison. Probably the easiest way to filter out bad people from your life. My phone rang maybe once every two weeks when I first got out, but when it rang, I was excited because I knew only good people had my new number.

"Surround yourself with those who only lift you higher."
– Oprah Winfrey

"You're a product of your environment, surround yourself with the best."
"Walk with the dreamers, the believers, the courageous, the cheerful, the planners, the doers, the successful people with their heads in the clouds and their feet on the ground."
– Wilfred Peterson

"Surround yourself with people who have dreams, desire, and ambition; they'll help you push for, and realize your own."
"If you surround yourself with positive people who build you up, the sky is the limit."
– Joel Brown

"People inspire you, or they drain you —pick them wisely."
– Hans F. Hansen

"Keep people in your life that will change it for the better."
"Surround yourself with positive people who believe in your dreams, encourage your ideas, support your ambitions, and bring out the best in you."
– Roy Bennett

"Energy is contagious, positive and negative alike. I will forever be mindful of what and who I am allowing into my space."
– Alex Elle

"Do not expect positive changes in your life if you surround yourself with negative people."

"Funny how your quality of life improves dramatically when you surround yourself with good intelligent kind-hearted positive loving people."

"Keep away from people who try to belittle your ambitions. Small people always do that, but the really great make you feel that you, too, can become great."

– Mark Twain

Start Slow, Build a Routine

Crawl, walk slow, walk, walk fast, jog, run, sprint, and fly to the fucking moon. Once you're out, take it slow. Patience is the keyword here. Yes, it feels like you're behind and you've got to play catch up, but don't get overwhelmed with those feelings and act in a manner that leads to burnout. "Rome wasn't built in a day," and you're basically trying to build Rome here. It's going to take years, not months. Create your own path and watch your plans and dreams unfold. The early choices are important; choose them wisely... one moment, one minute, one day at a time.

The early days are crucial for forming a strong foundation and positive momentum. Try to keep the days simple at first with only a few items on your to-do list, don't overwhelm yourself or work yourself into a frenzy and exhaust your mind and body. Keep it simple for the first weeks and months; maybe just work, p.o. meetings, and exercise. Then slowly add things in once you get into a rhythm and have built a disciplined and healthy daily routine. Don't forget to do mental and emotional health checks and routine maintenance.

Make exercise the pillar of your daily routine. In doing so, you create a healthy bedrock and keystone habit, and you also surround yourself with other healthy individuals. You can even become part of a community as well.

2¢ When I got out, I started slow. Really slow. I barely left the house for the first few days, institutionalized? Maybe. All I did at first was check-in with the P.O. and ride a bike around the neighborhood to get familiar with it. I went to the Plaid Pantry at night to get some snacks, but nothing too crazy cause I only had $250 when I got out. About a week out, I started applying for jobs and after 2-3 weeks I joined a gym. After I secured a job, I joined the MMA gym. I did the lifting gym early afternoon and MMA in the evenings and mornings on weekends. It was work and gym, that's it, and it was like that for a long time.

I started by adding one thing into my day. Once that became established and I felt good about my routine, I added in something new. My phone probably went 10 days without ringing and I was cool with that. I didn't give my number out to anyone except for work or my good buddies from home. Whenever my phone rang I knew it was either important or a positive person. I've kept it that way so whenever my phone rings, I'm excited about it. After about a year I was comfortable with my routine and path trajectory so I started allocating some time and energy into dating. There came a point when the relationship took more energy than I was cool with and had to break it off. I started out slowly, and everything that got added into my routine was closely scrutinized and extremely calculated.

"The two hardest tests on the spiritual road are the patience to wait for the right moment and the courage not to be disappointed with what we encounter."
– Paulo Coelho, *Veronika Decides to Die*

"Trees that are slow to grow bear the best fruit."
– Molière

"He that can have patience can have what he will."
– Benjamin Franklin

"When the same old routines in your life give you the feeling, that somewhere down this path you've lost yourself. When the beginning of a new day seems dreadful and lacks true purpose. You are not alone, but you alone can fix this. Pray for purpose, and fight to find it. There are things in this world you have always wanted to do, no matter how big or small. Get out there and do them. Most of the battles we fight in life are with ourselves."
– Ron Baratono

Linear vs. Exponential Growth

Linear: Arranged or extending in a straight line. Progressing from one stage to another in a single series of steps.

Exponential: An increase becoming more and more rapid.

Know the difference between these two types of growth, and realize that your own path in life can either follow the path of linear growth or the path of exponential growth. Both are fine but try to view yourself and your vision for yourself in terms of a chart. I consider those that choose a career and plan to work for the same company to be linear. They can expect regular raises and promotions if they put in the effort and commitment. The person on the exponential path is still going to have to get a job, but it is seen more as a means to get income to invest in their side hustle. Early on in the progression, those on the linear path will seemingly surpass those on the exponential path. They will begin to get raises or promotions in the first couple of years, whereas those on the exponential path will probably quit and start different entry-level jobs to fit into their schedule and allow time to work on their true goal. If they stick with it and become successful, those on the exponential path will eventually surpass those on the linear path in a spectacular fashion.

Linear vs. Exponential

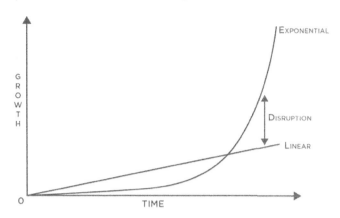

Source: Salim Ismail, Michael Malone and Yuri Van Geest, *Exponential Organizations* (New York: Diversion books, 2014).

<u>Getting a Job</u>

Trading in hours of your life to pay for shelter, food, and life's necessities is just a reality of the world. Unless you can find a way to bypass the work part, it usually has to become a priority. The goal is to eventually turn your passion into the thing that will pay for all of life's necessities, but at first, you'll probably have to grind it out with a job you don't really like. The trick is finding a job that somehow fits into the bigger picture of your ultimate goal. You don't have to take the first job that comes your way; choose one that can somehow run parallel with or contribute to your goals. This way, you won't just be working to earn the income necessary to survive; you'll also be building skills that add value to you and can aid you in your future endeavors.

2¢ One of my dreams is to build my own house someday, so I looked for a residential construction job thinking that I'll get paid while learning how to build a house. I learned carpentry, plumbing, electrical, and drywall. Most importantly, I learned how to build things. This gave me skills in the prototyping and inventing world. I later used the skills I learned from my construction job to become an inventor. I didn't necessarily love my job, but it gave me a skillset that made me way more valuable. I also know how to build a house now, so when I'm able to I can build my dream home.

Do your work and do it well, learn it, become better, more efficient, and get to the point where you are achieving the work without having to put much thought into it. Then you can devote your extra mental capacity toward your other goals. Eventually, as time goes by, you're able to put more and more energy into your side hustle and dream purpose until it turns into your main hustle. This is where those annoying quotes about work not being work if you love it come from; it stems from not working as an employee for someone else's dream, but working toward your own.

2¢ I worked construction and welding for years. I built up my fabrication and building skills to the point where I can basically build anything I want. I reinvested all my extra income into my side project by building prototypes and a website. Eventually, the day came when my side project became my main source of income, and I no longer had to work construction anymore. I envisioned it in my mind, and three summers in a row I said to myself, "This is the last summer I'll be working labor." I didn't give up, and last summer my side project popped off to the point where I no longer have to work labor. What a satisfying feeling!

If you get a job where you can wear headphones while you work, you can listen to shit and work productively at the same time. With a subscription to Audible, you can become educated on any subject you desire. Find a subject that interests and intrigues you, peruse the selections and titles, read the reviews, find books that prime your thirst for knowledge, and delve into learning and educating yourself. You can give yourself an education that is specifically catered to what your passions and interests are simply by listening to "How-to" books, biographies, podcasts, etc. while you work. You can get the same education as a PhD without having to pay for tuition by listening to and reading the same books that they study in universities.

2¢ One of my greatest passions is self-help books. While working the various construction gigs, I was always listening to something - a new book or repeating a previous one. I used to share my titles with a buddy, and finally one day he says, "Dude, I'm not really into those self-help books." I was in shock. How could you not love this shit? A few months later, I mentioned to him that I started writing this book. He said, "Ohhh, that's why you're always listening to those books, for research." I did not see it like that. I didn't view my passion for self-help books as research; I just loved listening to them. But looking back, it was like research… I picked something up from every book, and eventually, I came up with my own self-help book. In a way, this entire book is just my mix-tape version of all my favorite self-help books.

Take pride in your work and become an asset. Don't burn any bridges, especially when you leave one job for another… You never know when you might need to fall back on an old income source or get a good reference.

"Knowledge is the new money, get you some."
– Eric Thomas

"Start by doing what is necessary, then do what is possible, and suddenly you are doing the impossible."
– Francis of Assisi

Law of Attraction

The law of attraction - A universal principle that states you will attract into your life whatever you focus on. Whatever you give your energy and attention to will come back to you. When you focus on the abundance of good things in your life, you will attract more positive things into your life. Conversely, if you focus on negative and bad things, you will attract negativity into your life. Simply put, what you put in, you get out. The things you think about and do end up becoming you, so be aware and mindful of your thoughts and actions all the time. Choose wisely who you hang around with. If you want to be a good, healthy person, surround yourself with good, healthy people. If you hang out with drug addicts and dealers, you will very likely be a drug addict or dealer.

Jack Canfield - Living the Law of Attraction

The law of attraction is the most powerful law in the universe. Just like gravity, it is always in effect, always in motion, and it is working your life at this very moment.

Like attracts like. If you are feeling excited, enthusiastic, passionate, happy, joyful, appreciative, or abundant, then you are sending out positive energy. On the other hand, if you are feeling bored, anxious, stressed out, angry, resentful, or sad, you are sending out negative energy. Through the law of attraction, the universe will respond musically to both negative and positive vibrations. It doesn't decide which is better for you; it just responds to whatever energy you are creating and gives you more of the same.

You get back exactly what you put out there. Whatever you are thinking and feeling at any given time is basically your request to the universe for more of the same, because your energy vibrations will attract energy back to you with the same frequencies. You need to ensure that you are continually sending out energy, thoughts, and feelings that resonate with what you want to do and experience. Your energy frequencies need to be in tune with what you want to attract into your life. If love and joy are what you want to attract, then the vibrational frequencies of love and joy are what you want to create. Think of it this way: it's a lot like transmitting and receiving radio waves; your frequency has to match the frequency of what you want to receive. You can't tune your radio to 98.7 on your FM dial and expect to get a station broadcasting on 103.3. It just won't happen. Your energy has to synchronize with or match the frequency of the sender, so you have to keep your vibration tuned to a positive frequency to attract positive energy back to you.

We have taken a look at just how powerful our thoughts and emotions are. We've discussed the importance of releasing the negative and staying in a positive emotional state of attraction in order to be a vibrational match for our dreams and desires. We've acknowledged the amazing agility of our subconscious mind and the importance of utilizing its unlimited potential to help us attract and create the lives we have only dreamed of in the past. We've also taken the time to define our purpose, dreams, and goals, and to clarify what it is that we want to attract into our lives. Now that you understand a little bit more about how you participate in the process of the law of attraction, you can begin to take responsibility for everything that you are currently attracting into your life. Now that you're aware of the role you play in creating your life, you can no longer create your future accidentally or by default. Take this to heart because this is your moment, your time to begin consciously, intentionally, and deliberately participating in the creation of the future you desire.

By now you have a pretty good idea of who you are, who you want to be, and where you want to go in life. You have a clear vision of what it is you want to do, be, and have. You have a desired outcome in mind now, a destination, and you will want to focus on this desired outcome. It's a lot like programming an internal GPS system to your chosen destination. Now that you know where you want to go, the universe will guide you there through the law of attraction. [20]

2¢ I always mention to people what I'm working on and what I'm trying to achieve. I reveal to them a goal I'm working on or whatever it is I'm stuck on. It never ceases to amaze me how helpful most people are. Many times, after mentioning a goal to an almost stranger, they say, "Oh you should check out so and so," or, "I know somebody that could help you with that." Whenever this happens, I always try to get a name and number and follow through on the tip. I'll start the convo out like, "I got your number from so and so and they mentioned you might be able to help with _____." I've found that most people like helping people, and this is the true essence of the law of attraction. Putting out into the universe what you want to happen and then watching it unfold in ways you'd never imagined.

"To accomplish great things, we must not only act but also dream, not only plan but also believe"
-Anatole France

"The universe is change, our life is what our thoughts make."
– Marcus Aurelius Antoninus

"Here's the problem. Most people are thinking about what they don't want, and they're wondering why it shows up over and over again."
"Are you a hoarder of more negative thoughts or positive ones? Whichever ones you hoard, grow into trees and then forests."
– John Assaraf

"Whatever the mind of man can conceive and believe, it can achieve."
– Napoleon Hill

"If you want to be happy, make someone else happy. If you want to find the right person in your life, be the right person. If you want to see change in the world, become the change you want to see."
"When you make a choice, you change the future."
"Everything that is happening at this moment is a result of the choices you've made in the past."
"The secret of attraction is to love yourself. Attractive people judge neither themselves nor others."
– Deepak Chopra

"Every thought we think is creating our future."

"The thoughts we choose to think are the tools we use to paint the canvas of our lives."
"I deserve the best, and I accept it now."
"The Law of Attraction requires that we focus our attention on what we do want, rather than what we don't want."
– Louise L. Hay

Manage Expectations and Emotions

Be aware of the emotions you're going to feel when you get out, and be prepared to feel them. Expectations can be very dangerous. This is commonly talked about in drug rehab for a reason. Chasing your dreams and having high expectations can be dangerous for someone that isn't mentally prepared for setbacks and failure. Continue doing the difficult mental health exercises, and never set yourself up for such a big letdown that it takes you down entirely. Try to separate yourself and who you are from the things you are trying to achieve. Maintain a strong sense of self and identity that is separate from your job and your endeavors.

Don't give up. Yes, failure and setbacks are difficult, but if you don't give up, they become guides and learning experiences. Once you adopt a positive and growth-focused mindset, you can almost instantly become aware that you're encountering a setback or tough situation. Instead of getting overwhelmed and overtaken by negative thinking, you can snap into action with positive thinking. Say to yourself, "Okay! I'm in one of those moments that is hard, how can I turn this into a positive? How can I use this to my advantage? How can I learn from this? How can I make some fucking lemonade here!?"

MANIA / DEPRESSION CHART ILLUSTRATION

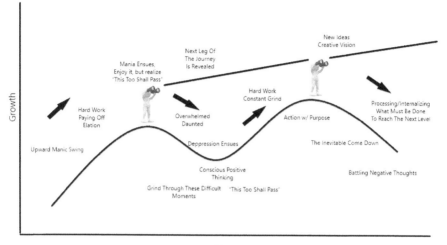

This illustration depicts the ups and downs of business and life in general. Growth and time are characterized by constant ups and downs. If you have a positive growth mindset, your highs will get higher and last longer, and your lows will be shorter and easier to get through.

Imagine you're stuck inside a mountain range. Using your best instincts, you decide which way you will travel to get out and you pick a mountain peak. It is hard, grueling work getting up to the top, and you hope you will see civilization or a way out when you reach the top. Once at the top, you get really excited; you can see so much more from up there, and using the elevated view, you can decide on the best direction to find your way out. But the high is short-lived; on the way down, you realize just how far you have to go to get there, and you start wondering, "If I get there, will it even be worth it? Or will it turn out that I took the wrong way?" On the bottom, it's tough; everything seems so far away, negative, and everything just sucks.

It's crucial to remain positive and keep grinding your way out because lying around sulking or getting high or drunk is not going to help. So, fuck all that shit —keep grinding through it. Life is full of ups and downs. Enjoy and use the highs, grind your way through the lows, and remember, it's all temporary. Always try to keep a positive mental attitude through it all.

"The capacity to surmount failure without being discouraged is the chief asset of every person who attains outstanding success in any calling."
– Napoleon Hill

Self-Discipline

Self-Discipline- The ability to control one's feelings and overcome one's weaknesses; the ability to pursue what one thinks is right despite temptations to abandon it.

Doing what you know you should do, even when you don't want to, and not doing what you know you shouldn't do, even when you want to.

Discipline is the key to self-mastery. The Flux Capacitor for success. The main motherfucking course. Without discipline, it's near impossible to achieve your goals and dreams. Without discipline, you'll likely give into impulsive and destructive behavior. Without discipline, you'll likely live a miserable and unhappy life and wind up back in prison. Simple as that.

"Life's easy when you live it the hard way and hard when you live it the easy way."
– David Kekich

The paradox of discipline —always doing things that make you feel good makes you hate yourself and contributes to low self-esteem. Doing things that you don't really want to do but are good for you makes you happy and builds your confidence, self- respect and self-worth. That whole "fuck it, I'm going to do what makes me feel good and happy in the moment" is bullshit. A good rule to live by when making decisions is having an honest conversation with yourself in the moment: "If I do this now, how will it affect the me of tomorrow, of next week, next month, next year, or the me on my deathbed?" A great example of this would be when you are confronted with an opportunity to do your drug of choice. Yes, in that very moment, it will make you feel good, it will temporarily numb away your problems, but think of you tomorrow; you will have just fucked your tomorrow self over big time. The you of tomorrow will be weakened; you will likely give in after that, you will be hungover or fiending, you will be down on yourself, you will hate yourself for relapsing, you will have lowered self-esteem and self-respect, and it will set off a chain of events that goes in the wrong direction and takes you off track. Conversely, if you make the decision that benefits the you of tomorrow, you will have reinforced the neural pathway that makes good and positive decisions; you will feel good about it, love yourself for it, and further yourself on the path that leads to purpose and achieving your goals. Glory awaits!

2¢ Out of all the virtues, this is the hardest for me. It really highlights the omnipresent battle in my head, the side of me that wants to be an extraordinary achiever versus the little bitch in me. I've always wanted to be an early riser, part of the 5am club. I will do good for a few days in a row then screw up and it messes with my self-talk, self-respect and self-esteem. I am still working on it. Some mornings I'm able to just jump out of bed and get to it, other times I just want to lay there and be warm and comfortable and hide from the world… the problem is when I do that I feel like shit and I start the day out with a loss. It's such a better start to the day to get that first "W" and create some positive momentum. I know deep in my heart that when I get my self-discipline dialed in I will be truly unstoppable. I work out 6-7 days a week and have a lot of entrepreneurial ventures so I do have a somewhat high level of discipline, but it can always be better, it can always be built on. I have found that, falling into complacency and rewarding myself with a break is the enemy and it never works out well. Discipline is surely the ultimate key to success and happiness.

"Discipline is the foundation upon which all success is built. Lack of discipline inevitably leads to failure."

"We all must suffer two things: the pain of discipline or the pain of regret or disappointment."

– Jim Rohn

"NO MORE. No more excuses. No more: "I'll start tomorrow." No more: "Just this once." No more accepting the shortfalls of my own will. No more taking the easy road. No more bowing down to whatever unhealthy or unproductive thoughts float through my mind." "There is only hard work, late nights, early mornings, practice, rehearsal, repetition, study, sweat, blood, toil, frustration, and discipline."
– Jocko Willink

Instant Gratification vs. Delayed Gratification

Instant gratification - The desire for and pursuit of immediate pleasure or reward without considering the long-term consequences. It is the tendency to prioritize immediate satisfaction over long-term goals or commitments. Instant gratification can be a hindrance to personal development and success, as it often leads to short-term gains at the expense of long-term goals.

Delayed gratification - The practice of resisting the temptation of immediate pleasure or reward in order to achieve a greater reward or benefit in the future. It is the ability to forgo immediate gratification in order to achieve long-term goals or commitments. Delaying gratification is a key factor in achieving personal success and happiness, as it allows individuals to invest in their future and achieve greater levels of personal fulfillment.

Being disciplined gives you the ability to abstain from negative things you may have urges to do, or to do things you may not want to do but should. Having discipline allows you to avoid a life of instant gratification. A life without discipline often leads to taking shortcuts and giving in to impulsive decisions that lead to misery. Exercise is a great way to begin building discipline when locked up. Everyone wants to feel good. But wanting to feel good right now all the time just isn't possible or sustainable. The harsh reality of life is that good times and bad times make up life; feeling good at times and feeling bad at times is just part of it. When you just want to feel good *now,* no matter the circumstances, you begin chasing instant gratification. Like when you want to get high after hearing bad news, so you can relieve the pain and feel good in the moment. This is not the way. Sometimes things happen, and you don't feel good, but that's okay: that's a normal part of life. If you find yourself feeling unhappy in a certain situation, allow yourself to feel it, honor it, work through it, try to discover the root of the bad feeling, and then decide how you can think and act to not feel that way anymore.

Delaying gratification is the ultimate path to feeling good. Continue delaying gratification until you are swimming in the rewards. Yeah, it feels good to go and buy things, but it's just a momentary dopamine hit. Soon after, you'll look at the item you purchased, feeling empty and hollow inside. And if you want to be rich, you're now that much further away from your goal. Save and delay gratification until you are filthy rich, that is the way.

Dopamine

Dopamine: The chemical that causes you to feel good and happy. When you use drugs, you get dopamine hits. This is how and why people get addicted to drugs, they do it for the dopamine hits, 'cause it feels good. Meth, heroin, cocaine, alcohol, sex, eating, and anything else that "feels good" gives you an instant dopamine hit. If you chase these dopamine hits, you will always end up having to do more to get the same dopamine as the first time. All these behaviors and actions give you a shortcut to dopamine.

The trick is to work hard for your dopamine hits. Achieving your goals and having a disciplined, slow, and steady rise in life gives you a balanced, measured, and healthy amount of dopamine that you have to work for and earn. Get dopamine produced by your own positive actions instead of dopamine introduced externally by a drug or destructive behavior. Earn your dopamine the hard way. There are no shortcuts. Shortcuts to dopamine are bullshit and always end badly.

"Willpower is what separates us from the animals. It's the capacity to restrain our impulses, resist temptation —do what's right and good for us in the long run, not what we want to do right now. It's central, in fact, to civilization."

– Roy Baumeister

Faith

Faith: A strong belief or trust in something or someone without requiring proof or evidence. Belief that you take action and calculated risks, things will work out in the end.

The type of faith discussed here is having faith in yourself, faith in the process. Feeling hopeful about your future; the faith that if you live courageously and fearlessly, take risks, and leap into chasing your dreams, everything will work out in the end. The ego does everything it can to keep you from taking risks and prevent you from failing in some way. Fear and doubt will never go away, no matter how far along you get on your journey. In the moments when you are stricken with fear and doubt, when the little voice is telling you to play it safe and not to do the things that you so deeply want to do, when no one believes in you or your vision, but you believe in yourself and that you're doing the right thing, that is faith. Whether you fear financial loss or public humiliation, in order to achieve your goal, you must have faith in yourself and the process. A deep belief that it will work out. And even if it doesn't and you end up failing, you know it is part of the process, a necessary step of your life with purpose and meaning.

"Faith removes limitations"
-Napoleon Hill

"If you sense your life's a mess right now, this is simply because your fears are just a little stronger than your faith."
-Robin Sharma, The 5 AM Club

2¢ I began developing faith while I was in prison and it really started growing after I got out. It started with me following through with the plans I had made in there. As I executed the plans I had made and things started unraveling, my confidence grew and although I was completely overwhelmed and daunted, I began developing a strong sense of faith that if I just kept on going things would work out. The more I did, the more I put myself out there, the more faith I got. The hard work I put in started paying off as small goals were being achieved. These days, I'm operating on pure faith. I have concrete knowledge that I am on the right path and I'm going to achieve my big goals. I just know it. Sure,

I still struggle with self-doubt, insecurity and fear, but they do not affect my decisions and hold me back like they once did. Now they are just annoyances that are dealt with swiftly. Taking the initial leap, going all-in on something, taking (business) risks and having faith that it will work out is such a rush. It makes me feel so alive. Going all-in is so stimulating that it has completely replaced my urge to use drugs. Taking life and business risks is truly my anti-drug.

This following excerpt by Napoleon Hill is timeless and one of my favorite takes on the type of faith I'm describing.

Napoleon Hill, 17 Principles of Success

"The active motivating faith that you can put into daily practice without regard to any form of theology or religion. The only religion I intend to deal with is the broad general religion of right thinking and right living as you meet the important human relationships in the real situations of life. The real difficulty in defining faith is that it is a state of mind and not a passive state of mind at that where the mind is merely giving assent but an active state of mind. The mind is in the state of relating itself to the great external along vital or vital force of the universe you see the word faith is what is known as an abstract idea or a purely mental conception that's why it is not better understood."

"Faith without work is dead. The emergencies of life often bring men to the crossroads where they are forced to choose their direction: one road being marked faith and the other, fear. What is it that causes the vast majority to take the fear road? The choice hinges upon one's mental attitude, the man who takes the fear road does so because he has neglected to condition his mind to be positive, but if you have failed in the past, so what? So did Edison, so did Henry Ford, the Wright brothers, Andrew Carnegie, and all other great American leaders who have helped to establish the American way of life with the aid of the light that shines from within. These are all truly great men that have recognized temporary defeat for exactly what it is: a challenge to greater effort backed by greater faith. Just the same as a single drop of water out of the ocean is an integral part of the ocean, know that

you too are a part of the universal purpose of infinite intelligence, so repeat these words: "I have complete faith and trust in infinite intelligence and I know that I am achieving my goals."[21]

"Trust the soup."
"Letting go of the things you cannot control and learning to trust the process."
- Steven Pressfield

"Again, you can't connect the dots looking forward, you can only connect them looking backwards. So you have to trust that the dots will somehow connect to your future, you have to trust in something; your gut, destiny, life, karma, whatever because believing that the dots will connect down the road will give you the confidence to follow your heart, even when it leads you off the well-worn path and that will make all the difference."
- Steve Jobs

"Desire backed by faith knows no such word as impossible."
- Napoleon Hill

Positive Mental Attitude (PMA)

The art of having a PMA is realizing that literally every situation you encounter, and every little choice you make, brings positive opportunities your way, whether obvious or hidden. There is an art and psychology of identifying the positive route and acting on it. This is the backbone of success, rolling with whatever comes your way and finding the best possible outcome. Being able to control your mind and thoughts so well that everything is a possible opportunity for advancement or growth.

It is inevitable that setbacks, obstacles, or "bad" and stressful situations are going to arise. They always do, and often at the worst possible time. If you aren't mentally and emotionally secure and prepared for them, they can be enough to send you into a tailspin. When this happens, the first and most important thing is to remain calm. Do not panic, do not lose your temper, and do not decide to say "fuck it" while you run from the situation by getting high. Breathe, think through it, be logical, and *stay positive*. Realize "this is one of those moments," then begin thinking about how you can turn the situation into a positive one. Maybe it forces you to do something you're not entirely comfortable with or ready for in your mind. Whatever the case may be, there is always an opportunity for growth and improvement, or some type of lesson hidden in it. Become a pro at turning everything into a positive, this is the art of having a Positive Mental Attitude.

"With every disappointment, heartbreak, or failure, there exists an equal (usually greater) positive benefit."
– Napoleon Hill

"How do I deal with setbacks, failures, delays, defeat or other disasters? Actually I have a fairly simple way of dealing with these situations, it is actually one word to deal with all these situations, and that is "Good"... When things are going bad, there is going to be some good that's gonna come from it. Unexpected problems? Good, we have the opportunity to figure out a solution. That's it, when things are going bad, don't get all bummed out, don't get startled, don't get frustrated, no, you just look at the issue and you say "good." Focus on the good. Take that issue, take that problem, make it something good."
– Jocko Willink

"Having a positive attitude isn't wishy-washy, it's a concrete and intelligent way to view problems, challenges, and obstacles."
– Jeff Moore

"Nothing can stop the man with the right mental attitude from achieving his goal; nothing on earth can help the man with the wrong mental attitude."
– Thomas Jefferson

"Positive thinking will let you do everything better than negative thinking."
– Zig Ziglar

"Optimism is a happiness magnet. If you stay positive, good things and good people will be drawn to you."
– Mary Lou Retton

"Keep your face always toward the sunshine —and shadows will fall behind you."
– Walt Whitman

"Whatever we face, we have a choice: will we be blocked by obstacles, or will we advance through and over them."
– Ryan Holiday, *The Obstacle Is the Way*

Synopsis

Before I went to prison, I always had big dreams, ideas, and aspirations. I always felt like I was destined to live an extraordinary life. My low self-esteem and self-limiting beliefs prevented me from pursuing anything meaningful or stepping outside of my comfort zone. It led to depression, self-loathing, and self-hatred. The chemical use I developed early in my teenage years as a form of escape from difficult emotions led to being used to cope with and numb the fact that I wasn't doing shit with my life. I wasn't chasing my dreams or setting goals, I was just getting high and hating myself for not doing anything. In prison, when I did the death exercises, I realized I was full of regret for not doing or trying things... I was full of regret for not "going for it." As I sobered up, I was hit with the worst feeling that I was wasting my life. As my sentence moved along, the pain of not trying heavily outweighed my fear of trying something and failing. I knew that taking business risks and taking a shot at doing something big would be the only way I'd have any self-respect moving forward. I spent my time healing from unresolved traumas, finding forgiveness, confronting my shadow, dissecting my fears, doubts and insecurities. I rewired my brain and adopted a growth mindset; I began my journey of self-mastery. Every day I would spend time meditating, mustering courage, and making pacts with myself to act in a way that I would not feel regret at the end of my life. I made a deal with myself that I would take business risks and risk failing at something, risk public ridicule and humiliation... that I would "go for it" when I got out. Prison was by far the most positive and important experience of my life. It was the turning point. It was exactly what I needed. The mindset I developed in there is the best thing that ever happened to me.

Last Words

I did two years, went in at 29, got out at 31. When I got out, I was worried that I'd never find a job and that society would be hard on me and my felonious status... that I'd never fit in again. It was all bullshit. The first job I applied for I got. After a week, I realized it wasn't what I wanted and I quit and got another job.

I had convinced myself that I didn't have what it takes to make it in the "business world." I thought the only way I was ever going to "make it" was with my decent athletic ability and mental toughness. The dream I held onto during my two years was to be an MMA fighter. Although I bet I could've done okay at it, I decided after roughly a year of training that I was too old and didn't want to put my body through that. Some might say this is an example of me giving up. I did give up on the MMA dream that I held onto while I was locked up, but only after giving it serious effort. The only reason I was okay with letting go of my MMA dream was because there was a new dream to replace it. My first dream evolved into something new, it was something that evolved after my making a genuine effort on my initial dream.

In the process of joining that gym and practicing Jiu Jitsu, Boxing, Muay Thai, and doing CrossFit 4-5 hours a day, I came to the realization that I was capable of doing whatever I wanted. Telling myself I didn't have the ability to make it in the "business arena" was more bullshit and doubtful, faulty thinking. A lie I told myself and believed for a short while. I learned through my attempt at chasing the MMA dream that anything I put my mind to is possible. Yeah, there's truth to that cheesy saying.

After suffering from torn rib cartilage and a concussion, I decided I didn't want to be a fighter anymore. But I also began believing in myself on a different front; the dream didn't die, it evolved. Through the process of joining that gym and going for it, my self-confidence and faith in the process grew and I started thinking that I wanted to become a serial entrepreneur. I began studying Stoic philosophy and self-help books. I had creative ideas for products... I began playing with prototyping and learning how to apply for patents, how to design websites and build a business. I listened to podcasts daily on how to do all these things, I was hungry as fuck. It took years, but I designed, invented, and launched a fitness product that I sell direct-to-consumer. I wrote this book and I'm working on multiple products at the moment as well as continuing to run and grow the first startup. But it all started with that decision to go for it initially; join that gym, and walk in there and say, "I'm going to be an MMA fighter." The most important part is that you show up and give it real effort. I never felt so uncomfortable walking through those doors the first time, but I kept showing up, I became a part of the community, made friends, met girls, discovered my learning style and that there's a learning curve to everything.

I also discovered the role that patience, persistence, discipline, determination, faith, courage, and PMA play in trying anything difficult. When it got really tough and doubts and negative thoughts arose, I would fall back on the pact I made with myself in there; to never give up, never go back to the old me, and to always keep on trying. I've been out five years; I'm sitting at a breakfast diner eating pancakes and drinking coffee while I write this. I remember two years ago I would hit this breakfast diner before my construction job and there was a burning desire in me to be a writer someday. I dreamed of a life where I could eat at a breakfast diner every morning without having to break my back for work. I am currently living my dream. Life is what you make it. If you live with intent, have clearly defined values and goals, know exactly what you want in life and why, then there's no reason you can't have the life you dream of. You can use your mind creatively to figure out how to get it and the passion and grit in your heart to overcome obstacles and roadblocks. Use this time to develop the best version of yourself and plan a life you can be proud of. Get out, chase your dreams and never go back!

"When the pain of not trying is greater than the perceived pain of trying and failing, then you are likely to try something new."
-Brene Brown

"When you want to succeed as bad as you want to breathe, then you'll be successful."
– Eric Thomas

"The worst thing one can do is not try, to be aware of what one wants and not give in to it, to spend years in silent hurt wondering if something could have materialized —never knowing."
– Jim Rohn

"If you're going to try, go all the way. Otherwise, don't even start. This could mean losing girlfriends, wives, relatives, and maybe even your mind. It could mean not eating for three or four days. It could mean freezing on a park bench... It could mean derision. It could mean mockery —isolation. Isolation is the gift. All the others are a test of your endurance, of how much you really want to do it. And you'll do it, despite rejection and the worst odds. And it will be better than anything else you can imagine. If you're going to try, go all the way. There is no other feeling like that. You will be alone with the gods, and the nights will flame with fire. You will ride life straight to perfect laughter. It's the only good fight there is."
– Charles Bukowski, *Factotum*

Resources

1- www.ncbi.nlm.nih.gov/pmc/articles/PMC1466870/
2- https://www.tokenrock.com/articles/all-healing-is-really-self-healing/
3- https://www.blissfullight.com/en-us/blogs/energy-healing-blog/what-does-heal-ing-really-mean
4- wildginger.my/what_healing_really_is
5- https://chat.openai.com/ what is the ego
6- https://chat.openai.com/ what is the subconscious mind
7- Negative Emotions list – compiled using Wikipedia definitions
8- Trauma Chapter 10 -Love, Boundaries, and Forgiveness
9- *infiniterecovery.com*
10- The Ultimate Character Traits List (benjaminspall.com)
11- *55 Positive Emotions (liveboldandbloom.com).*
12- https://www.viacharacter.org/character-strengths
13- https://www.tcnorth.com/building-confidence/12-benefits-increasing-self-confi-dence
14- https://www.tcnorth.com/building-confidence/12-techniques-to-build-self-con-fidence/
15- https://en.wikipedia.org/wiki/Andrew_Carnegie
16- How To Own Your Own Mind. Napoleon Hill. September 2017. Publisher: Tarcherperigee
17- The War of Art: Break Through the Blocks and Win Your Inner Creative Battles. Steven Pressfield. April 2003. Publisher: Warner Books (NY)
18- https://www.mayoclinic.org/tests-procedures/cognitive-behavioral-ther-apy/about/pac-20384610
19- https://medlineplus.gov/benefitsofexercise.html
20- Jack Canfield's Key to Living the Law of Attraction: A Simple Guide to Creating the Life of Your Dreams. Jack Canfield. December 2007. Publisher: Hci
21- Napoleon Hill's Keys to Success : The 17 Principles of Personal Achievement. Na-poleon Hill. October, 1997 Publisher: Penguin Publishing Group
22- https://en.wikipedia.org/wiki/AQ
23- https://en.wikipedia.org/wiki/Social_intelligence
24- Endsley, Mica; Jones, Debra (2016-04-19). Designing for Situation Awareness (Second ed.). CRC Press. p. 13. ISBN 978-1-4200-6358-5.
25- https://en.wikipedia.org/wiki/Situation_awareness

Josh Bryant and Adam benShea

With innovation and dedication prisoners make incredible strength gains.

Jailhouse Strong offers functional strength training with a workout system that is based on the training habits cultivated behind bars.

Through interviews with personalities ranging from a former Mr. Olympia, who started lifting behind bars, to a co-founder of the Crips street gang, Jailhouse Strong describes the workouts prisoners use to become lean and powerful.

Jailhouse Strong includes programs for lifting, bodyweight movements, and conditioning with unarmed combat techniques. The workouts require minimal cost, equipment, time, and space and they can be done at home, in a hotel, or just about anywhere.

Whether you are doing 10–25 or working 9-5, Jailhouse Strong can fit into your schedule because Jailhouse Strong provides the fitness habits that are crucial for getting strong and for maintaining a level of emotional balance amidst the volatile reality found on both sides of prison walls.

Josh Bryant has held world records in powerlifting and won the Strongest Man in America title in 2005. Now, he is referred to as the "trainer of the superstars" because he works with some of the world's strongest and most muscular athletes at Metroflex Gym in Arlington, Texas, and via the Internet. To contact Josh about seminars, online coaching or to sign up for his free training tips newsletter, visit www.JoshStrength.com.

Adam benShea is a Brazilian Jiu-Jitsu black belt and has won the California, Pan Am, and World Championships. He teaches Brazilian Jiu-Jitsu and is a college lecturer on California's central coast.

II - A Brief History of Jailhouse Strength

Prisons have existed since the beginning of civilization, because humans have always wanted to separate criminals from law-abiding citizens. Early jails were different from the societal reintegration institutions of today. They were merely a place to hold individuals until the real punishment could be carried out. In early prisons, there was no pretense of rehabilitating the inmates; just keeping them out of society until the gallows were ready to go; like a holding pen at the slaughterhouse.

Prisons did not change much until the late eighteenth century, when American Benjamin Rush lobbied for prison reform in Pennsylvania. Rush asserted that the primary objective of punishment should be the reformation of the criminal, and deterrence from future crime. He argued for a change in punishment philosophy because the incarceration experience tended to harden criminals, and engendered hatred toward the government.

As a result of Rush's work, prisons gradually became what they are today, or claim to be: rehabilitation facilities. In accordance with this goal of rehabilitation, prisons started to offer recreational programs and activities to help the prisoner acclimate into a civil society. One of these activities was weightlifting. Proponents of weightlifting in prisons say that "banging around the pig iron" helps the inmates pass the time, relieve stress and anxiety, build a sense of purpose, and create a positive self-image. They also say that prisoners who lift will behave better because they do not want to lose their access to the iron. Some prison administrators, like Garry Frank, believe that weightlifting not only helps the individual inmates, but also the institution as a whole, because it creates a safer population. Frank, the athletic director at Angola State Prison in Louisiana, asserts that the low rates of violence at his prison may be attributed, in part, to the inmates being able to lift weights.

Historically, one result of correctional facilities allowing weightlifting was the image of a muscled mountain of a man emerging from an iron-barred cave. A behemoth who did fit this stereotype was the "Scranton Superman," Jim Williams. During the 1960s, Jim began lifting while incarcerated in Rockview State Correctional Institution in Pennsylvania. While in the pen, Williams started to experiment with high-volume training and lifting twice a day, concepts which were way ahead of his time. He also found ways to overcome the Spartan setting of the prison weight room. For example, when he needed a weight belt to lift, he would tie a couple of towels around his waist. Even without state-of-the-art equipment, Williams still went on to become the second man in history to officially bench press 600 pounds. He was also built like a brick shit house; he was said to have a 60-inch, relaxed chest, and 23-inch cold-measured arms!

Another strong man that came out of the can was Greg "the Beetle" Lowe. Greg is considered one of the greatest power lifters of all time, a feat he achieved while being locked up in the State Correctional Institution in Graterford, Pennsylvania. Although the Beetle did not start lifting seriously until he got locked up in 1985, it only took him eight years to become the national champion. As he aged, this incredible strength stayed with Lowe. In 2007, at the age of 52, the Beetle competed in a powerlifting meet and squatted 865 pounds, bench pressed 460 pounds, and deadlifted 820 pounds for a 2,145-pound total! Amazingly, he did all this while serving a life sentence.

A dedicated focus on training while incarcerated can lead to international success, as it did for some of the Japanese-Americans who were in the internment camps of World War II. While being detained in the Tule Lake Segregation Center, Emerick Ishikawa introduced a number of young men to physical culture through the Tule Lake Weightlifting and Bodybuilding Club. After the war, Ishikawa became a US Champion and a bronze medalist in the World Weightlifting Championships. However, it was one of his pupils, Tommy Kono, who would become one of the greatest lifters of all time. Before he medaled at three Olympics, won six consecutive World Weightlifting Championships, and set 21 world records, Kono began his lifting career at an internment camp with a York Ten-In-One exercise kit purchased by Block 27 of Ward II.

A discussion of successful jailhouse training in a Spartan training environment would not be complete without a reference to the Soviet Gulags.

During the Commie days of Russia, Stalin sent millions to work and die in the Gulag. Even faced with this dire situation, the Gulag prisoners were known to do brutal kettlebell workouts as a means to maintain physical strength, and their sanity. This tradition continues in the Russian prisons of today with the holding of the "Spartakiada Games," a prison Olympics of sorts. This competition brings together nine Siberian prisons to compete in six different events. In 2011, the winner of the most prestigious event, the kettlebell overhead press, performed 67 reps with a 24-kilogram (52.8 pounds) kettlebell in each hand.

Although these stories indicate a vibrant iron culture behind bars, over time, many members of the general public began to fear the "super criminals" they felt were being created in the prison weight pile. This general fear and public outcry pressured many politicians and prison administrators into reassessing the benefits of jailhouse lifting. Consequently, by the early 1990s, some states began to phase out their weightlifting programs. Arizona was the first to completely get rid of their weight room, and other states quickly followed suit.

As a result of states banning the lifting of weights and removing traditional exercise equipment, prisoners began to create incredibly interesting exercises by just making use of what they had. They had bunks, so they did pull-ups on them. They had floor space, so they did pushups, sit-ups, and burpees. They had a deck of cards, so they did "Tyson squats" (explained below).

Even without access to quality training equipment, some beautiful physiques were developed. What this taught us, and what was confirmed with our numerous interviews, is that state-of-the-art equipment is not needed to create a magnificent shape.

All you need is a plan and a work ethic.

This book will provide you with the plan. You have to provide the work ethic.

Progression

One day, the no-nonsense powerlifter, Steve Holl, took a cursory glance around his training grounds. Then he said, "Look around this gym. The same people lifting the same weights, doing the same exercises, and looking the same for the past 15 years." After a slight shake of his head, he added: "If you take one thing away from today, remember, you gotta put more weight on the bar. No matter what you do, you have to put more weight on the bar."

If you don't progressively overload your training, you will not make gains in size, strength, and muscularity. In the case of bodyweight exercises, by doing 100 push-ups in every workout, you will eventually cease making gains. Once your body has adapted to the workout, you will need to add more reps, sets, time under tension or added resistance. Resistance can be as varied as your cellmate on your back, or a weighted vest; anything to make the exercises more difficult. Even if it is as small as decreasing your rest periods from 45 seconds to 43 seconds, that is still progress. You are still getting better.

Cons are always striving to outdo other cons and destroy their own personal records. Do the same.

To make progress toward jailhouse strength, follow these four principles of progress:

The Principle of Individual Differences: Everyone cannot and should not train in the same manner. As one becomes more advanced in training, his ability to recover from workouts will change, and the gains he makes from different types of training will evolve. Some people are fast gainers, while others are slow gainers; most fall somewhere in the middle. Genetics, experience, aging, injuries, supplementation, mental acuity, and a host of environmental factors will influence how each person adapts to training. This applies to you as you experiment with different routines in this book. The more information you track, the more effectively you can decipher what works best for you.

The Principle of Overcompensation: This is a very simple principle, but its importance is often overlooked. It is a survival trait built into your DNA by your Creator. The way that your body adapts to stress metamorphoses into strength. A scar or callus is an example of your body trying to heal itself as efficiently as possible. When you put an increasing amount of stress on your muscles, they will overcompensate by becoming bigger and stronger as a defense mechanism.

The Law of Overload: Whether it means more reps, sets, shorter rest periods, additional weight added to your body, or increased frequency, the principle is to progressively make training more intense. If you do not continually overload your training, you will either maintain or, more likely, lose ground. We are either evolving, or devolving. Choose to evolve!

The Importance of Deloads: More is not always better, because you want to gradually overload your training. Periods of very intense training must be followed by lower intensity periods, also called "deloads." This may be referred to as an active recovery.

Sleep and Recovery

Many convicts are able to get a full night's sleep, and take naps throughout the day. Sleep is imperative to recovery. The body produces most of its natural growth hormone during REM sleep. While many experts state the body needs at least seven hours of sleep, they are talking about the "average person." If you are a hard-training athlete, you are not average, and you need more sleep than this. At least eight hours of solid, uninterrupted sleep is recommended, along with taking naps as often as possible.

A recent study conducted by the University of Chicago Medical School, and published in the *Annals of Internal Medicine*, confirmed the importance of a full night's sleep. The study consisted of two control groups, in which members of both groups were on calorie-restricted weight loss diets. One group was sleep deprived; the other group had a full night's sleep every night. Both groups lost the same amount of weight in this study; however, the sleep-deprived group had 25 percent less fat loss. If you are trying to maximize muscle mass and minimize body fat, you need your sleep.

Convicts certainly have an advantage by not having to work 40-plus hours a week... Here are some steps that you can take as a free man to increase your sleep quality. Remember to use your time wisely. The irony for most free men is that your free time is minimal.

Pray or meditate before bed. It is comforting to be at peace with your Creator and/or the world around you

Avoid the use of alcohol, tobacco, and caffeine (and other stimulants like cocaine and ephedrine)

Sleep in a dark room

Read before bed

Take melatonin

Eat dinner by candlelight versus electrical light

Get a massage or use a foam roller prior to going to bed

Set a sleep routine

Take a nap during the day

Remove stress from your life (if you are a worrier, journal your thoughts before bed)

Avoid good or bad news before bed; emotional stimulation will keep you awake

IV - Bodyweight Strength Training

Behind bars, an individual encounters many potential obstacles standing in the way of an ideal training environment. Specifically, he has limited time outside, minimal space, and, often, a lack of access to workout equipment. These obstacles may be the same as those faced by the time-crunched executive, the stressed Mr. Mom, or the energy-depleted college student. Yet, the hardened inmate does not let these minor situational difficulties impede his progress toward getting Jailhouse Strong.

Using your bodyweight as resistance is one of the best ways to construct a workout program that will not be affected by these slight inconveniences. This is because a bodyweight workout can be completed anywhere, and without equipment. With the correct application of the Jailhouse Strong bodyweight workouts, the street soldier and the weekend warrior alike can make real gains in functional strength and construct the broad-shouldered, lean-waisted look that elicits immediate respect and prolonged feminine stares at the community pool.

Bodyweight exercises have many advantages over traditional exercises like, the clichéd dumbbell curl, or the fitness machines that are the darlings of late-night infomercials. For example, bodyweight movements are considered closed kinetic chain exercises. In "yard talk," a closed kinetic chain exercise is one in which *you* move, while an open kinetic chain exercise is one in which the *weight* moves. A bench press is an open kinetic movement because your effort moves the *weight* (attached to a bar) up and down. A push-up is a closed kinetic movement because your effort moves your *body* up and down.

Closed kinetic exercises can be more beneficial in terms of results and safety, because they build functional strength and are easier on your body. Closed kinetic movements are able to build functional strength because they train the body to move its own weight, a prerequisite for almost any real-world activity, from lifting yourself off your couch, to transitioning into a liver punch. Closed kinetic exercises are considered safer, because they allow an individual's body structure to determine the movement pattern of the joints. This allows for a more natural range of motion that may remove excessive stress from the joints, and enables the muscles to perform the workout. With this natural range of motion, joints are less likely to be injured, and muscles are more likely to grow.

In addition, most bodyweight exercises are classified as compound exercises, which mean that they are multi-joint movements that work several muscle groups simultaneously. Performing big compound exercises (as opposed to small, isolated movements) can produce big muscles and release a large amount of anabolic hormones (the primary building block for gaining strength, increasing sexual desire, and changing that sagging jaw-line to a chiseled countenance).

With the Jailhouse Strong approach to bodyweight strength training, lack of funds or training equipment are no longer legitimate excuses for not reaching your fitness goals. The only excuse is a lack of desire! With the discovery of the Jailhouse Strong bodyweight exercises, you become the master and commander of your fitness destiny.

Below are some of the push-up variations that are most beneficial for building functional strength, for pushing your way to the front of the chow line, or through the rampant BS at your next sales convention:

Regular Push-ups: Pretty self-explanatory (remember high school gym?). Keep your back straight, your palms flat on the ground, and get a full range of motion.

Diamond Push-ups: These hit your inner chest and build your back arms (triceps). Place your thumbs and forefingers of each hand together to form a diamond. (Note: If this variation causes elbow pain, use the traditional narrow-hand placement variation of the push-up.)

Wide Push-ups: Place your hands beyond shoulder-width to build slabs of rocks over your delts and pecs. (Note: If you have a history of shoulder problems, you may want to avoid this movement.)

Knuckle Push-ups: As old-school MMA fighter Ken Shamrock says, "Knuckle push-ups make you punch harder." If you line up your clenched fists horizontally (thumbs pointing toward each other) the push-up movement will better mimic the punching movement.

Clap Push-ups: Descend as in a normal push-up, but on the way up, press explosively and clap your hands together. This variation develops explosive strength that has carryover into prison yard brawls and quick exits from the dinner table with that annoying ex.

Explosive Push-ups: If you are new to Jailhouse Strong training, you may not be ready for clap push-ups. Start with an explosive push-up. Begin in a traditional push-up position, descend and then explode up to have your hands leave the floor.

Hindu Push-ups: *Used by nineteenth-century Indian champion wrestlers and twentieth century Japanese shootfighters, Hindu push-ups epitomize functional combat strength. Begin with your feet wide, your butt in the air, your head down, and your hands shoulder-width apart. Descend down and then up, with your head up and your eyes looking upward toward the ceiling. Return to the starting position and repeat the movement. Remember to keep your elbows tucked in through the push-up.*

Fingertip Push-up: *Forget the Kung-Fu grip; these will build the Jailhouse Strong vice grip! Like a regular push-up, but only the tips of your fingers are touching the floor.*

Decline/Elevated Push-up: *Hit your lower chest by putting your palms on the floor and your feet on an elevated surface, like a chair or your bunk. The steeper the decline, the more your chest will be worked, because the elevated angle forces you to handle a greater percentage of your bodyweight. Unlike with weight training (where a decline press is easier than the traditional bench press), a decline push-up is much more difficult/advanced than a traditional push-up.*

Incline Push-up: *Hit your upper chest with your feet on the ground and your hands on any elevated surface. While an incline press in weight lifting is more difficult than a bench press, an incline push-up is much easier than a regular push-up. In fact, the steeper the decline, the easier the push-up will be. If you are having difficulty with the regular push-up, the incline push-up may be your gateway to the process of push-up mastery.*

Deficit Push-up: *Usually this push-up is done with three chairs, but it can be done with a bed or two stacks of the paperbacks inmates read to get through what seem like endless hours. Whatever you use, get the raised platforms on roughly the same level. Put your feet together on one elevated surface and your palms on the other two surfaces that are shoulder-width apart. On the downward portion of the push-up, dip your chest below the raised platforms. This will offer a deep stretch and offers a core* strengthening benefit as long as you keep your back straight. For those coming from a powerlifting background, these push-ups build starting strength for the bench press. (Note: If you have a history of shoulder problems, avoid this movement.)

Deck of Pain: A favorite of street soldiers and hardened cons, the deck of pain is a way to use the slick gambler's favorite tool for more than just Five Card Stud. Take a 52-card deck and shuffle the cards so that you have no idea what card will come up next. Flip the first card and do however many push-ups the card says. So, for numbered cards, do whatever number of push-ups coordinate with the number on the card. For picture cards (jack, queen, and king) do ten push-ups. And, for the aces do eleven push-ups. Once completed, you will have done 380 push-ups. For the deck of pain neophyte, shoot to complete the deck in under 15 minutes.

Below are some of the most common pull-up variations, and some unorthodox ones as well.

Pull-up: The classic pull-up is executed with palms wrapped around the bar and facing away from the body. On the bottom of the exercise, the arms are fully extended. Pull your body up, squeeze your back, open your chest and get your chin over the bar. After which, lower yourself back to the starting position.

Chin-up: The little brother of the pull-up, the only difference being that the palms are facing you. This slight difference will allow a better pump for the attention-getting and T-shirt-popping biceps. When it comes to the meat and potatoes of bodyweight bicep exercises, the chin-up is the filet mignon.

Alternate grip- With one palm facing you and one facing away, pull yourself up and above the bar. The benefit of the alternate grip is that this hand placement mimics the grip most often used in grappling (a common element of almost every real unarmed combat conflict).

Commando: Grab the bar like a baseball bat and pull yourself alongside your ear until the bar hits your traps. Then, repeat on the alternate side.

Triangle: *Hang at full extension with a traditional grip. Pull yourself at a diagonal angle toward your left hand until your chin is above the bar. Keeping your chin above the bar, move your body toward your right hand. Then, take a diagonal descent down and return the starting position to complete a downward-facing triangle. One of the many benefits of this pull-up is that it increases the period during which the back muscles are under tension.*

Hercules chin-up: *A creation of the Jailhouse Strong system that uses incremental movements to build monster knots (biceps). Pull yourself up until your chin is over the bar and hold for two seconds. Then, descend halfway down and hold for two seconds. Then repeat this movement for the prescribed number of repetitions. Finish with arms fully extended at the bottom.*

Pyramid: *A one hundred pull-up workout is the type of training that builds the type of broad back that veteran street soldiers, combat athletes, and even some office drones will recognize as the mark of the functionally strong. An approachable way to bang out a century of pull-ups is by way of a pyramid. Start with one pull-up, then perform two, and continue until you reach ten pull-ups. After hitting ten pull-ups, work your way back down the pyramid to one. If this pyramid is too audacious for you, a pyramid could be done at any number.*

Dips: *Although traditionally done on a dip bar, behind-bars prisoners have been known to do dips off a bed, or on two stacks of books. Any stable object can be used as placement for your hands. Lower yourself until you reach a ninety-degree angle at your elbows, then return to full extension. Leaning forward with your upper body will provide a larger load, and greater workout, for the chest and front delts, while keeping a straight back shifts the focus of the workout to your triceps. In traditional dips on a bar, your feet are suspended in the air. In a modified version, your feet may be placed on the ground or, for more of a challenge, they can be elevated on a chair or bench. The wide range of possibilities for performing dips makes them a perfect workout for the compressed space of the individual doing ten to twenty years, or the traveling salesman on the road for seven to ten days.*

Handstand Push-Ups: Few things scream Jailhouse Strong and functional power like a pair of marble slabs for shoulders. Without weight, handstand push-ups offer the best way to develop the shoulders. For those new to the movement, place the back of your head near the base of a wall, put your hands alongside your head (fingers pointing toward the wall), and then kick your feet into the air until they reach the wall. From this inverted position, perform a push-up.

Triceps Extensions: Many ex-cons have said that the biggest back arms they ever saw were on the prison tier. Triceps extensions are a bodyweight method for building horseshoe back arms that fill out prison denim, work-man wool, or preppy polo. Prisoners have been known to use the iron bar on the end of their bed, while inner-city bodyweight training enthusiasts use a portion of their local playground. Whatever you use, the basic mechanics of the exercises are consistent. Grasp a horizontal bar at the mid-torso range, then place your forehead against the bar and walk your feet backward until your body is at an angle. Then press your bent elbows to full extension. For a greater challenge, walk your feet farther out.

Lower Body:

Although the lower body is often neglected by the all-show-no-go, spray tan types, those looking to be Jailhouse Strong know that a powerful tree has strong roots. Building the roots of your tree can be done away from the gym, and outside of the squat rack.

Hindu Squats: Used for centuries by the great Indian champion wrestlers, Hindu Squats build muscularly thick upper legs. Begin with your legs roughly shoulder-width apart, and slowly descend down. Look to control the movement so that your muscles, not gravity, are doing the work. Your goal should be to have your butt break ninety degrees, but do not let your knees fall too far over your toes, because this offers the potential of injury. Once you have hit the bottom, return to the starting position at a controlled pace. Another key point is to inhale on the negative (going down) and exhale on the positive (going up). One version of the Hindu Squat is sometimes called the "prisoner squat," with the only real differences being that the practitioner's fingers are interlocked behind his head (execution victim-style) and the feet remain flat in the prisoner squat.

Jumping Squats: *Like the Hindu Squat, except that once you hit the bottom of your squat, your explosive movement upward is continued into a jump. This exercise builds explosive power and, when done in high reps, explosive strength endurance.*

Pistol Squats: *Sometimes referred to as a one-legged squat, pistol squats are done by placing a leg straight in front of you, and squatting with the other leg. The straight leg should remain as rigid possible. This movement develops balance, along with strength.*

Jump and Tuck*: Descend into a quarter-squat position and push your arms behind your body, then reverse the motion by swinging your arms upward and jumping as high as possible. In the midst of jumping as high as possible, pull your knees toward your chest. Return to the ground in a quarter-squat position to absorb some of the force of the landing, and reduce potential stress on the knees (do not let your knees fall over your toes). After returning to standing upright, you can progress through multiple repetitions in rapid-fire succession for an effective plyometric workout that requires no special-ized equipment. (Note: You may want to avoid this movement if you have a history of knee problems.)*

Lunges: *A functional movement for unarmed combat that replicates the body mechanics of shooting a wrestling takedown, or transitioning from striking to grappling, lunges have tremendous value in generating aesthetic and utilitarian strength. The traditional lunge is done by standing with your feet shoulder-width apart and then stepping forward with one leg and bending at the knee. After which, you return to the starting position and perform a lunge with the opposite leg. When performing this exercise, cer-tain measures should be taken to reduce the chance of injury: keep the back straight, the eyes looking forward, and do not let the lead knee fall over your toes.*

Back Lunge: *Like the traditional lunge, except you step backward to perform the movement. This causes an increased focus on the glutes, or what some prisoners call the "booty."*

Side Lunge: *A sidestepping variation of the traditional lunge that works the inner thighs and adductors.*

Jumping Lunge: *A dynamic version of the traditional lunge that builds explosive strength by jumping, instead of stepping, the foot forward and back to the initial position.*

Calf Raises: *While aesthetic appeal falls low on the Jailhouse Strong priority list, calf raises build calves that would be the envy of any Santa Monica personal trainer. To perform this exercise, stabilize your body by placing your hands against an immovable object like a wall (or the shoulders of your three-hundred-pound cellmate). Then, raise your body onto your toes. As you progress in strength, work toward using less of your toes, and eventually supporting your bodyweight on just the big toe of each foot.*

Wall Sit: *When in prison, time is the most common commodity. Use this commodity to purchase isometric strength in the lower body by placing your back against a wall, and lower your body until you are sitting in an imaginary chair. With your knees bent at a right angle, hold this position to build enduring leg strength. More advanced versions of this exercise include lifting your toes off the ground, or lifting your heels off the ground.*

Tyson Squat Workout:

Mike Tyson came back to boxing from his three-year stint in a correctional facility bigger and broader. Along with T-shirt-popping biceps, and shoulders that could take out door jambs, Tyson's upper legs (quadriceps and hamstrings, for those of a scientific bend) filled out his trademark black trunks like never before. To develop these tree trunks, it is said that Tyson's leg workout during his time behind bars was the following:

Start with ten cards and line them up 2-4 inches apart. Squat and pick up the first card, then move to the next card and place the first card on top of the second card. After which, you squat twice more to pick up each card individually, before moving to the third card. Walk to the third card and squat twice to stack each card, then squat three times to pick up each card before carrying the cards to the fourth card, and proceeding with the pattern. You will continue this pattern of individually stacking and picking up the cards until you move through all ten cards in the line. At that point, you will have completed 100 squats. You can add cards as your strength and endurance increase.

Core:

Core strength is not just valued by Pilates instructors. Building core strength is an essential component of any training program, because your core connects the strength in your lower body to the strength in your upper body, and can provide vital defense against body blows, and much worse. The hard reality of real core training is that is must be done with the goal of protecting your internal organs from a blunt force strike, or to minimize the damage of an edged weapon. Leave the late-night infomercials and catchy gimmicks to the suburban housewife who is nobly searching for the high school body that will remain just beyond her reach, and remember that few routines will build real power in the midsection like the Jailhouse Strong core routine. Of course, this routine is done with functional strength as the goal, but it will also help to flatten flab and cut up abs. As a means to strengthen your core from every angle (front, back, and side), a wide range of core strengthening movements are included in the Jailhouse Strong program.

Hanging Leg Raises (knees up): Jump up, grab a pull-up bar, and hang until your body is motionless. While flexing your lats and abs, ensure that your arms are straight. Bend your knees and in a controlled fashion (2 seconds up and 2 seconds down), raise your knees to your chest, and return to the starting position. Along with the benefits to your core, leg raises also strengthen your back and grip.

Hanging Leg Raises (obliques): Hanging motionless from a pull-up bar, bend your knees, and slowly lift them up to one side (as high as possible). This movement is accomplished by curling your midsection from the bottom up, not by forcefully jerking your knees. At the top of the movement, squeeze your lower abs and side abs for a one count. In a controlled manner, repeat the movement on the opposite side. Rather than relying on momentum, the key to this exercise is to make your abs do the work.

Hanging Leg Raises (straight leg): These are performed like the bent knee raises, but your legs are locked out straight (90 degrees) as you lift them in a controlled manner to belly level. Return to a straight hang in a controlled manner.

Hanging Leg Raises (to bar): This is a more advanced version of the straight leg raise. Rather than bringing your straight legs just to the belly level, progress until your feet touch the bar. Remember to raise and lower your legs in a slow and controlled fashion.

Windshield Wipers: This is probably the most difficult of the leg raise variations. Hang from a pull-up bar and bring your straight legs up until they touch the bar. From this position, rotate your straight legs side to side (like a windshield wiper). This exercise uses isometric contractions that increase one's ability to absorb a body shot, and has a rotational component which is beneficial for building the powerful twisting motion utilized in many strikes and takedowns. In addition, it tones the obliques and trims down love handles.

Crunches: Like gym class, put your hands behind your ears or crossed over your chest. Cross your feet and raise them off the ground. From there, the movement should revolve around the portion of the exercise where tension in the abs is greatest.

Bicycles: Start in a crunch position and alternate touching opposite elbows and knees.

Flutter Kicks: Raise your head off the ground, lift your feet six inches from the floor, and place your hands under your butt. Then, alternate lifting each leg. This movement builds strength in the lower abs and hip flexors.

Scissors: Begin in the same position as the flutter kick exercise, then alternate crisscrossing one leg over the other.

Touch Ankles: To strengthen the upper abs, place the soles of your feet on the ground and back flat on the floor. Rise to touch your ankles.

Alternate Touch Ankles: Alternate touching each ankle to build strength in the obliques.

Plank: A static exercise that strengthens the core while building isometric strength through the upper and lower body, the plank offers much benefit to the Jailhouse Strong practitioner. To execute, distribute the weight of your body between your forearms and your toes, and make sure that focus is paid to keep the abs tight.

Side Plank: Hit the obliques by resting your body on one forearm and the side of the same side foot (with the other foot stacked on top). The opposite arm may be placed on the hip, or pointed straight in the air.

Plank Walk-up: A dynamic and more advanced version of the traditional plank. Begin in the regular plank position. Place one hand at a time into a push-up position. Once in the starting position of a push-up, return to the traditional plank one hand at a time. This variation of the plank offers strength building benefits to the core and the upper and lower body.

100 Burn: An approachable way to track the progress of your Jailhouse Strong core routine is to start with the "100 Burn." Perform the first seven exercises for 10 repetitions, and the last three for a count of 10 seconds, as a means to reach a total count of 100. The first goal in this routine should be to gradually increase the repetitions and the count until a total of 1,000 is reached.

Workouts:

Jailhouse Method (reverse pyramid) - The Jailhouse Method may be done with any type of bodyweight exercise in a descending order of repetitions. The Jailhouse 20 is a total of 210 total repetitions, where set 1 is performed with 20 repetitions, set 2 is 19 repetitions, set 3 is 18 repetitions, etc. Each set descends by one less repetition. A Jailhouse 30 is a total of 465 repetitions. After each set is performed, walk 16 feet (8 feet across your cell and 8 feet back).

Juarez Valley Method – Like the Jailhouse Method, the Juarez Valley Method may be done with any type of bodyweight exercise. Unlike the Jailhouse Method, the Juarez Valley Method offers alternating ascending and descending reps. Repetitions are performed in descending order on all odd-number sets, but repetitions are performed in ascending order on even-number sets. In the middle, they meet! A Juarez Valley 20 is performed liked this:

Set 1 - 20 reps	Set 11 - 15 reps
Set 2 - 1 rep	Set 12 - 6 reps
Set 3 - 19 reps	Set 13 - 14 reps
Set 4 - 2 reps	Set 14 - 7 reps
Set 5 - 18 reps	Set 15 - 13 reps
Set 6 - 3 reps	Set 16 -8 reps
Set 7 - 17 reps	Set 17 - 12 reps
Set 8 - 4 reps	Set 18 - 9 reps
Set 9 - 16 reps	Set 19 - 11 reps
Set 10 - 5 reps	Set 20 - 10 reps

The complaint about the Jailhouse Method is that the difficulty in the beginning of the workout can be overwhelming, and that the ease at the end of the workout is not challenging. In contrast, the Juarez Valley Method keeps a steady level of difficulty throughout the workout.

Total Repetition Method – Similar to the previous methods, the Total Repetition Method may be done with any type of bodyweight exercise. However, the chosen exercise is performed in the fewest number of sets to hit the prescribed amount of repetitions. Using the Total Repetition Method,100 pull-ups might look something like this: Set 1 - 15 reps, Set 2 - 12 reps, Set 3 - 11 reps, Set 4 -10 reps, Set 5 - 10 reps, Set 6 - 9 reps, Set 7 - 8 reps, Set 8 - 7 reps, Set 9 - 7 reps, Set 10 - 6 reps, Set 11 - 5 reps.

V - Burpees

Burpees are an old-time jailhouse favorite. But before they became the favorite exercise of inmates, they gained popularity during World War II as a way to evaluate the strength, endurance and agility of the soldiers of our finest generation. The value of burpees for the everyman comes from specific movement patterns and joint angles that allow one to work virtually every muscle in the body.

To get a little scientific, all of the different muscles and movements involved in burpees cause the exercise to be classified as a compound, multi-joint movement. As a compound, multi-joint movement, burpees enable the production of more testosterone than a more isolated exercise (like a dumbbell bicep curl). The benefits of a rise in testosterone include increased muscle mass, and a decrease in body fat. Generally, burpees are performed in sets, or intervals, which are more effective than traditional aerobic training for fat loss. By upping the intensity of the burpee interval training, one can increase the aerobic benefit of burpees.

Turning away from muscle gain and fat loss and looking toward functional training, burpees engage almost every muscle and joint in your body. This forces your central nervous system (CNS) to work synergistically with your major muscle groups. Enhancing the combined effort will increase performance in any sport that requires multiple movement patterns and joint actions. Increased performance in movement pattern and joint actions improves activities ranging from cage fighting, to helping that hot coed with her luggage.

What is a Burpee?

If burpees are so great, why don't more people include them in their workouts? The reason is simple: No one makes money if you do burpees. Burpees do not require fancy equipment, a famous personal trainer, or membership in an elite fitness club. All you need is your body, and a minimal amount of space. The bottom line is that, unlike many fitness trends and programs, burpees do not benefit anyone but you. In its original form, the burpee was performed in four steps. However, since the 1940s, a plethora of variations have evolved. Therefore, the initial burpee became known as the "Four Count Burpee."

Executing a Four Count Burpee

Start in a standing position.

Count 1 - *Drop into a squat position and place your hands on the ground.*

Count 2 - *In one rapid motion, push your feet straight back into a plank (push-up position).*

Count 3 - *In one quick movement, again return to the squat position.*

Count 4 - *Return to the original starting position.*

Because the burpee is not limited by a machine or free weights, there are countless variations that can be done to increase intensity and difficulty. Here are just a few examples:

Burpee Push-up *–At the bottom push-up position, go on and perform a push-up. Performing one push-up would be known as a 5-count burpee. You can progress to more push-ups. Old time veteranos may consider diamond push-ups, Hindu push-ups or even one-armed push-ups.*

Mexican Burpee- *From the bottom push-up position, perform consecutive push-ups. As you get back to the start position, lift the left knee in the air, then the right knee. Adding knee lifts are great for building abdominal/core strength, and it has functional transference to street fighting by mimicking the delivery of a knee strike.*

Jumping Burpees- *Complete a regular 4- or 5-count burpee, then jump as high as possible before starting the next burpee. The addition of the jump builds explosive power and strength endurance. The benefits of increased explosion range from faster reflexes in a self-preservation scenario at the gas station at 3 AM, to clearing out of your office cubicle before the crowds ruin your happy hour.*

Broad Jump Burpees- *While these may be tough in the confines of your cell, you always have yard time. This is like a jumping burpee, but you don't jump up. Instead, jump forward as far as possible.*

Hurdle Burpee- *For this version, you perform a four-count burpee, then jump over an object. If an object is not available, jump up and bring the knees as high as possible into a jump tuck burpee.*

Pull-up Burpee- *After completing a burpee, jump up to a pull-up bar and perform a pull-up. An advanced version of this can be done with multiple pull-ups, or by adding a muscle-up.*

One-legged Burpee- *For those who are more advanced, bend at the waist and put your hands on ground so that they are in alignment with your shoulders. Now jump back with the standing leg to push-up position. Then jump forward with the one leg that was extended, and do a one-leg jump. Alternate sides. This movement can help eliminate asymmetrical physique blemishes and movement patterns. Also, this has direct transference to most real-life activities that require some kind of unilateral (one-limbed) balance.*

Old-school Blood and Guts 8-Count Burpee- *A burpee with a jumping jack on the ground. The eight-count movement is as follows: (Count 1) squat with your hands on the ground, (Count 2) kick your feet back, (Count 3) kick your feet out to form a Y shape, (Count 4) bring your feet back together, (Count 5) descend into the lower portion of a push-up, (Count 6) ascend into the upper part of the push-up, (Count 7) bring your feet back under you, (Count 8) jump straight up.*

Mountain Climber Burpee- *Do a traditional push-up burpee (5 count), but after performing the push-up, do two mountain climbers. This builds flexibility and abdominals of steel that protect your vital organs from blunt force trauma, and minimize the damage of makeshift edged weapons.*

Handstand Burpee- *For the real Sultans of Strength, perform a traditional 5-count burpee, but after the push-up, kick into a handstand, and then back down into push-up position, then, finish the movement of the burpee.*

Among the benefits of this variation are an increase in coordination and strength, and bowling ball-like deltoids.

Jumping Jack Burpee- *Similar to a jumping burpee, but after the initial vertical jump is performed, land and do five jumping jacks. Remember the jumping jacks in junior high school gym class? Nothing beats the basics.*

Pistol Burpee- *Do a jumping burpee, and upon completing the jump, land and do one pistol squat with each leg. The nature of this movement has benefits in a world where real life happens unilaterally (that is, you eat with one hand, throw a punch with one arm, kick with one leg, etc.).*

Lunge Burpee- *Do a four-count burpee followed by one lunge with each leg. The benefits of lunges range from stronger takedowns in a no-rules combat encounter, to tighter buns in a no-clothes bedroom encounter.*

Jailhouse Strong Baker's Dozen Routine

Like all of the Jailhouse Strong bodyweight movements, the following routine can be completed in your cell, your hotel room your office, or the extended bed of a pick-up truck. However, the 8-foot walk between sets was taken from the standard size of a correctional facility cell.

Performed in Descending order:

Perform 13 burpees
Walk 8 feet, turn around, and walk back to start.

Perform 12 burpees
Walk 8 feet, turn around, and walk back to start.

Perform 11 burpees
Walk 8 feet, turn around, and walk back to start.

Perform 10 burpees
Walk 8 feet, turn around, and walk back to start.

Perform 9 burpees
Walk 8 feet, turn around, and walk back to start.

Perform 8 burpees
Walk 8 feet, turn around, and walk back to start.

Perform 7 burpees
Walk 8 feet, turn around, and walk back to start.

Perform 6 burpees
Walk 8 feet, turn around, and walk back to start.

Perform 5 burpees
Walk 8 feet, turn around, and walk back to start.

Perform 4 burpees
Walk 8 feet, turn around, and walk back to start.

Perform 3 burpees
Walk 8 feet, turn around, and walk back to start.

Perform 2 burpees
Walk 8 feet, turn around, and walk back to start.

Perform 1 burpee
Walk 8 feet, turn around, and walk back to start.

Once completed, you will have banged out 91 burpees. As a goal, finishing the above routine (using four-count burpees) in 12 minutes is above average, 10 minutes is very good, and with 8 minutes you are on your way to Sultan of Strength status. Once you can complete the above routine in 8 minutes or less, it is recommended that you use more advanced burpee variations. Some inmates like to go back up the pyramid in ascending order from 1to 13. If you can do the Jailhouse Baker's Dozen in both directions in under 18 minutes, you are a bad ass.

Prisoner Burpee Challenge: *The Prisoner Burpee Challenge is a son of a buck! Like the Baker's Dozen, it is performed in descending order. While it may seem redundant to include this program, it is included because there are established norms that you can shoot for, and eventually shoot to demolish!*

Perform 20,19,18,17,16,15,14,13,12,11,10,9,8,7,6,5,4,3,2,1 burpees. However, these burpees are six-count, and they require a push-up and jump. Complete this as fast as possible. Below 25 minutes = good, below 22 minutes = excellent, below 18 minutes = you own the yard and the warden will call you "Sir."

Tabata Burpee Routine *: Any exercise can be incorporated into the Tabata training! The basic outline of the Tabata training method is as follows:*

4 minutes long

20 seconds of intense training (in this case as many burpees as possible)

Followed by 10 seconds of rest

Done for a total of 8 sessions or rounds

The Tabata protocol can start off with one round. It is not meant to be paced, but rather, it should be a frenzy of fitness fury. Start off with one round, work your way to two rounds, then eventually top out at four rounds (taking a 1-minute break between rounds). This will make the goal workout 20 minutes in duration. If you can get 6 reps per interval you are in good shape. However, if you reach 8 reps per 10-second interval, you are in great shape, and will pretty much be conditioned to meet any type of volatile situation.

Tabata Burpee is one of the most intense High Intensity Interval Training (HIIT) workouts on record! Just four minutes in one round will increase metabolic rate, which in turn increases fat loss. Thus, it is a very time-efficient way to increase your ability for all high-intensity exercise, your anaerobic and aerobic capacity, and your mental toughness. Remember: Each set is balls to the wall because this is a sprint, not a marathon!

Burpee Progression

When you are slamming the pig iron it is easy to track progress. Put more weight on the bar, and you are stronger. You have to make progress in your bodyweight exercise and conditioning exercises as well. In regard to this, one of the first tenets learned in physiology is the principle of overload. This simply means that training must progressively increase in intensity over a period of time. Using the same reps, sets, frequency, training loads and methods will not result in increases in performance.

The Jailhouse Strong Baker's Dozen routine is a great place to start with a four-count burpee. It is a total of 91 burpees, with your goal being to make it in under 8 minutes. Then, you should progress to more difficult variations of the burpee. If all you ever did for exercises was burpees, you could continue to make physical gains, because we have provided a significant amount of exercise variations, rep schemes and way to increase intensity.

There are tons more routines. Be creative, decrease rest intervals, add reps, and add sets. Always challenge yourself to set personal records and outdo others!

VI - Bodyweight Workout Routines

Week 1 Day 1

Workout A (Explosive Power and Strength)

Exercise	Sets	Reps	Notes
Plyometric Push-ups	3	6	
Deficit Push-ups	3	5	Explode into air, use explosive power to get as high in the air as possible.
Hand Stand Push-ups	4		stop one shy of Failure.
One-armed Push-ups	3		stop one shy of Failure.
Decline Push-ups	3	8	Controlled down explode up.
Deficit Push-ups	3	8	One second pause at the bottom.

Workout B (Muscle Hypertrophy and Endurance)

These exercises are performed in a circuit to absolute failure, unless otherwise noted. Repeat this circuit four times.

Exercise	Sets	Reps	Notes
Hindu Push-ups	1	Failure	Entire circuit repeated 4 times.
Incline Push-ups	1	Failure	
Neck Bridges	1	1	Hold 30s
Decline Push-ups	1	Failure	Hold 30 seconds
Burpees	1	15	As you advance, choose more difficult variations.
Head Nods	1	25	
Leg Raises	1	15-20	

Week 1 Day 2
Workout A (Explosive Power and Strength)

Exercise	Sets	Reps	Notes
Jump Tucks	5	5	
Jumping Lunges	3	10	
Jump Squats	4	8	
Pistol Pause Squat	3	5	
Pause Prison Squats	2	10	Pause 3 seconds at bottom of the rep.
Jack Knife Sit-ups	5	12-16	

Workout B (Muscle Hypertrophy and Endurance)

Exercise	Sets	Reps	Notes
Tyson Squat Workout			Sets, reps vary greatly as you progress.
Prison Squats	8	Max	Do as many reps as possible in 20 seconds, rest 10 seconds, repeat for a total of 8 cycles.

Hindu Squats	1	Max	Continuous for 2 minutes straight. Do as many reps as possible in 2 minutes without stopping and maintaining good form.
Reverse Lunges	2	Max	Continuous for 30 seconds straight. Do as many reps as possible in 2 minutes without stopping and maintaining good form.
Lateral Lunges	2	50	
Lunges	3	20	
Plank	1	1	Hold for 30 seconds
Side Plank	1	1	Hold for 30 seconds. 1 set each side

Week 1 Day 3

Workout A (Explosive Power and Strength)

Exercise	Sets	Reps	Notes
Jumping Pull-ups	3	4	
Jumping Chin-ups	3	4	
Wide Grip Pull-ups	3	8	
Chin-ups	3	8	
Hercules Chin-ups	5	5	
Walk Talls	3	1	Continuously for 30 seconds.
Neck Bridges	3	1	Continuously for 30 seconds.

Workout B (Muscle Hypertrophy and Endurance)

Exercise	Sets	Reps	Notes
Chin-ups Juarez Valley 10	10	10 to 1	See description.
Jailhouse 8 Pull-ups	8	8 to 1	See description.

Hercules Chin-ups	5	Failure	
Inverted Rows	1	Failure	

Week 1 Day 4 Repeat Day 1
Week 1 Day 5 Repeat Day 2
Week 1 Day 6 Repeat Day 3
Week 1 Day 7 Off

Week 2 Day 1

Workout A (Explosive Power and Strength)

Exercise	Sets	Reps	Notes
Plyometric Push-ups	4	6	
Deficit Push-ups	4	5	Explode into air like a plyometric, use maximal explosive power to get as high in the air as possible.
Hand Stand Push-ups	4		Do as many reps as possible, stopping one shy of Failure.
One Armed Push-ups	3		Do as many reps as possible, stopping one shy of Failure.
Decline Push-ups	3	9	Controlled down explode up.
Deficit Push-ups	3	9	1 second pause at the bottom

Workout B (Muscle Hypertrophy and Endurance)

Exercise	Sets	Reps	Notes
Deck of Pain	52	1-11	See description.
Juarez Valley 20 Incline Push-ups	20	20 to 1	See description.
Diamond Push-ups	2	Failure	
Toilet Skull Crushers	2	Failure	Hold 30 seconds.

Neck Bridges	2	1	Hold 30 seconds.
Jailhouse Dozen Burpees	12	12 to 1	See description.
Head Nods	2	30	
Leg Raises	3	15 -20	

Week 2 Day 2

Workout A (Explosive Power and Strength)

Exercise	Sets	Reps	Notes
Jump Tucks	5	6	
Jumping Lunges	4	10	
Jump Squats	5	8	
Pistol Pause Squat	3	5	
Pause Prison Squats	2	15	Pause 3 seconds at bottom of the rep.
Jack Knife Sit-ups	5	12-16	

Workout B (Muscle Hypertrophy and Endurance)

Exercise	Sets	Reps	Notes
Tyson Squat Workout			See description, sets, reps vary greatly as you progress. Beat Week 1 time.
Prison Squats	8	Max	Do as many reps as possible in 20 seconds, rest 10 seconds, repeat for a total of 8 cycles.
Hindu Squats	1	Max	2 minutes straight. Do as many reps as possible in 2 minutes without stopping and maintaining good form.
Reverse Lunges	2	Max	50 seconds straight. Do as many reps as possible in 2 minutes without stopping and maintaining good form.
Lateral Lunges	2	60	

Lunges	3	30	
Plank	1	1	Hold for 30 seconds.
Side Plank	1	1	Hold for 40 seconds. 1 set each side.

Week 2 Day 3

Workout A (Explosive Power and Strength)

Exercise	Sets	Reps	Notes
Jumping Pull-ups	4	4	
Jumping Chin-ups	4	4	
Wide Grip Pull-ups	3	9	
Chin-ups	3	9	
Hercules Chin-ups	5	5	
Walk Talls	3	1	Perform continuously for 30 seconds.
Neck Bridges	3	1	Perform continuously for 30 seconds.

Workout B (Muscle Hypertrophy and Endurance)

Exercise	Sets	Reps	Notes
Inverted Rows	52	1 to 11	See Deck of Pain
Chin-ups	1	Failure	
Pull-ups	1	Failure	
Hercules Chin-ups	6	Failure	

Week 2 Day 4 Repeat Day 1
Week 2 Day 5 Repeat Day 2
Week 2 Day 6 Repeat Day 3
Week 2 Day 7 Off

Week 3 Day 1

Workout A (Explosive Power and Strength)

Exercise	Sets	Reps	Notes
Plyometric Push-ups	4	6	
Deficit Push-Ups	4	6	Explode into air, use explosive power to get as high in the air as possible.
Hand Stand Push-ups	4		Do as many reps as possible, stopping one shy of Failure.
One Armed Push-ups	3		Do as many reps as possible, stopping one shy of Failure.
Decline Push-ups	3	10	Controlled down explode up.
Deficit Push-ups	3	10	1-second pause at the bottom.

Workout B (Muscle Hypertrophy and Endurance)

Exercise	Sets	Reps	Notes
Juarez Valley 30 Push-ups	30	30 to 1	See description.
Incline Push-ups	2	Failure	
Jailhouse 10 Deficit Push-ups	10	10 to 1	See description.
Toilet Skull Crushers	4	Failure	
Neck Bridges	2	1	Hold 35 seconds.
Jailhouse Dozen Burpees	12	12 to 1	See description.
Head Nods	2	30	
Leg Raises	3	15- 20	

Week 3 Day 2

Workout A (Explosive Power and Strength)

Exercise	Sets	Reps	Notes
Jump Tucks	5	6	
Jumping Lunges	4	10	
Jump Squats	5	8	
Pistol Pause Squat	3	6	
Pause Prison Squats	2	15	Pause 3 seconds at bottom of the rep.
Jack Knife Sit-ups	5	12-16	

Workout B (Muscle Hypertrophy and Endurance)

Exercise	Sets	Reps	Notes
Tyson Squat Workout			Beat Week 2 time.
Prison Squats	8	Max	Do as many reps as possible in 20 seconds, rest 10 seconds, repeat for a total of 8 cycles.
Hindu Squats	1	Max	3 minutes straight. Do as many reps as possible in 2 minutes
Reverse Lunges	3	Max	60 seconds straight. Do as many reps as possible in 2 minutes
Lateral Lunges	2	80	
Lunges	3	44	
Plank	1	1	Hold for 45 seconds
Side Plank	1	1	Hold for 45 seconds. One set each side.

Week 3 Day 3

Workout A (Explosive Power and Strength)

Exercise	Sets	Reps	Notes
Jumping Pull-ups	4	4	
Jumping Chin-ups	4	4	
Wide Grip Pull-ups	3	10	
Chin-ups	3	10	
Hercules Chin-ups	5	5	
Walk Talls	3	1	Perform continuously for 45 seconds.
Neck Bridges	3	1	Perform continuously for 45 seconds.

Workout B (Muscle Hypertrophy and Endurance)

Exercise	Sets	Reps	Notes
Chin-ups	???	150	
Pull-ups	1	Failure	
Inverted Rows	1	Failure	
Hercules Chin-ups	6	Failure	

Week 3 Day 4 Repeat Day 1
Week 3 Day 5 Repeat Day 2
Week 3 Day 6 Repeat Day 3
Week 3 Day 7 Off

Week 4 Day 1

Workout A (Explosive Power and Strength)

Exercise	Sets	Reps	Notes
Plyometric Push-ups	5	6	
Deficit Push-ups	5	6	Use explosive power to get as high in the air as possible.
Hand Stand Push-ups	5		Stop one shy of Failure.
One-armed Push-ups	3		Stop one shy of Failure.
Decline Push-ups	3	12	Controlled down, explode up.
Deficit Push-ups	3	12	1-second pause at the bottom.

Workout B (Muscle Hypertrophy and Endurance)

Exercise	Sets	Reps	Notes
Deck Pain Push-ups	52	1 to 52	See description.
Jailhouse Baker's Dozen	13	1 to 13	See description.
Jailhouse 10 Deficit Push-ups	10	10 to 1	See description.
Juarez Valley 20 Push-ups	20	1 to 20	See description.
Toilet Skull Crushers	4	Failure	See description.
Neck Bridges	3	1	Hold 45 seconds.
Head Nods	2	50	
Leg Raises	3	15 to 20	

Week 4 Day 2

Workout A (Explosive Power and Strength)

Exercise	Sets	Reps	Notes
Jump Tucks	5	6	
Jumping Lunges	4	10	
Jump Squats	5	8	
Pistol Pause Squat	3	6	
Pause Prison Squats	2	15	Pause 3 seconds at bottom of the rep.
Jack Knife Sit-ups	5	12-16	

Workout B (Muscle Hypertrophy and Endurance)

Exercise	Sets	Reps	Notes
Tyson Squat Workout			Beat Week 3 time.
Jailhouse 20 Reverse Lunges	20	1 to 20	See description.
Jailhouse 20 Forward Lunges	20	1 to 20	See description.
Hindu Squats	1	Max	4 minutes straight. Do as many reps as possible in 4 minutes without stopping and maintaining good form.
Lunges	2	44	
Plank	1	1	Hold for 60 seconds.
Side Plank	1	1	Hold for 60 seconds. 1 set each side.

Week 4 Day 3

Workout A (Explosive Power and Strength)

Exercise	Sets	Reps	Notes
Jumping Pull-ups	4	4	
Jumping Chin-ups	4	4	
Wide Grip Pull-ups	3	12	
One Armed Chin-ups	3	3	
Hercules Chin-ups	5	5	
Walk Talls	3	1	45 seconds.
Neck Bridges	3	1	45 seconds.

Workout B (Muscle Hypertrophy and Endurance)

Exercise	Sets	Reps	Notes
Chin-ups Total Repetition Method	???	200	See description.
Pull-Ups	1	Failure	
Inverted Rows	1	Failure	
Hercules Chin-ups	3	Failure	

Week 4 Day 4 Repeat Day 1
Week 4 Day 5 Repeat Day 2
Week 4 Day 6 Repeat Day 3
Week 4 Day 7 Off

Take a week to deload after this. You can start over and up the intensity with the techniques described. This is a very intense regimen. Proceed with caution but remember that conventional programs get conventional re-sults. They don't make you Jailhouse Strong!

5 Days a Week OG Bodybuilding Program (for the serious bodyweight trainer)

This is a more advanced workout for those who have already built the base of their jailhouse strength.

Complete each exercise one repetition short of failure, and repeat the circuit for a period of 30-45 minutes. To ensure that muscles receive a break in the midst of this Jailhouse Strong bodyweight blast, perform the circuit in the order that the exercises are given. Once the prescribed number of repetitions are achieved, increase the amount of repetitions, or progress to more advanced variations. Do this routine for 8-12 weeks before switching to another Jailhouse Strong bodyweight workout.

Monday & Thursday

Exercise	Sets	Reps	Notes
Pull-ups	??	6-10	
Parallel Dips	??	8-15	Full range of motion, use no momentum to aid the movement.
Hercules Chin-ups	??	6-12	
Decline Diamond Push-ups	??	15-25	
Head Nods	??	30-60	
Walk Talls	??		30 seconds continuous.

Tuesday & Saturday

Exercise	Sets	Reps	Notes
Leg Raises	??	12-15	
Jack Knife Sit-ups	??	8-15	
Side Planks	??	1	Each side. Hold 30 seconds.
Tyson Squat Workout	??	??	Do as much as possible in 5 minutes, as you gain conditioning increase reps, do not add time.
Hindu Squats	??	30-60	
Lunges	??	12	
One Leg Calf Raises	??	20-30	Each side.
Jump Squats	??	8-12	
Jumping Lunges	??	8-12	

Wednesday

Exercise	Sets	Reps	Notes
Juarez Valley Burpee Routine	See Notes	See Notes	Do this for 12 minutes. If you get to a Juarez Valley 20, increase the difficulty of the burpee by, say, changing from the basic burpee to the Mexican variation.
Chin-ups	3	Failure	
Neck Bridge	2	1	Hold 1 minute.
Jailhouse Method Hand Stand Push-ups	??	??	Do this for 8 minutes. The goal is to work to a baker's dozen.
Deck of Pain Push-ups	52	1-11	No more than 15 minutes, stop at deck or 15 minutes, whichever comes first.
Pull-ups	2	Failure	

New Fish Routine: A "Fish" is a new inmate. So, this workout is for one who is looking to build a foundational level of jailhouse strength. Work set should be defined as one rep shy of failure.

Monday

Exercise	Sets	Reps	Notes
Push-ups	5	10-20	
Prison Squats	5	15-20	
Leg Raises	5	10-20	
Planks	3	1	Hold for 30 seconds.

Tuesday - Off

Wednesday

Exercise	Sets	Reps	Notes
Burpees	??	??	10 minutes, work as high as possible within 10-minute time frame.
Unarmed Combat Drills	??	??	Do drills for 10 minutes. Refer to Unarmed Combat Section.
Walking Lunges	3	??	Lunge for 20 yards straight, with as few as reps as possible.
Inverted Rows	3	5-15	

Friday

Exercise	Sets	Reps	Notes
Hindu Squats	5	20-40	
Chin-ups	5	5-10	
Diamond Push-ups	4	10-20	
Jack Knife Sit-ups	3	10-15	

You now have the roadmap for getting Jailhouse Strong. To illuminate your path, follow the Jailhouse Strong Five Decrees. On your journey toward acquiring new-found strength, remember these rules, and use them as a guide for staying the Jailhouse Strong course. A close adherence to these directives offers a way to achieve new-found levels of strength, confidence, and physical presence.

XI - Conclusion: The Jailhouse Strong Five Decrees

1. Get excited about training. In a jail, time can go real slow. There are no women, no night clubs, no beach...you get the idea. So, you need some-thing to excite you. For many, hardcore training offers a vessel to receive all their energy, intensity, and attention. They plan workouts and are con-stantly creative in constructing new ways to strengthen their bodies. In ad-dition, they let nothing stand in the way of training. It becomes the primary focus of their life. As a consequence, it offers a source of therapy, a means to develop a hardened body, and a tool for bettering themselves.

2. Get plenty of rest. Inmates sleep a lot, and on a regular basis. Their bod-ies become accustomed to the routine of sleeping at a specific time. This allows for recovery from training. Also, prison life offers an escape from many of the stresses associated with life on the outside (e.g. a hectic work schedule, a mortgage, traffic, etc.). The increase in rest and decrease in stress raises testosterone levels and accelerates recovery.

3. Eat meals at regular intervals. The body thrives on a routine. While the calories consumed by prisoners are not of the first order, they are con-sumed on a regular basis, and at a regular time. This allows for the body to depend on receiving muscle-building nourishment at a specific time.

4. Stick to the training basics. If there is one thing that you can take away from this book, it is this: you are born with everything you need to become Jailhouse Strong. By using bodyweight exercises, you can get broad, strong, and lean without equipment. If you do have access to a weight pile, train the core lifts.

5. Sorry. This rule could be seen as "Promoting Violence." (You'll have to look it up when you get out!)

Josh Bryant – Jailhouse Strong

The End

Made in the USA
Middletown, DE
27 August 2023

37433289R00099